Rational Theology As Taught By The Church Of Jesus Christ Of Latter-day Saints

RATIONAL
THEOLOGY

As Taught by the
Church of Jesus Christ of
Latter-day Saints

BY

JOHN A. WIDTSOE

Published for the Use of the Melchizedek Priesthood
by the General Priesthood Committee
1915

o

Rational Theology

As Taught by the
Church of Jesus Christ of
Latter-day Saints

BY

JOHN A. WIDTSOE

Published for the Use of the Melchizedek Priesthood
by the General Priesthood Committee
1915

Copyright, 1915
BY
JOHN A. WIDTSOE

PREFACE

A rational theology, as understood in this volume, is a theology which (1) is based on fundamental principles that harmonize with the knowledge and reason of man, (2) derives all of its laws, ordinances and authority from the accepted fundamental principles, and (3) finds expression and use in the everyday life of man. In short, a rational theology is derived from the invariable laws of the universe, and exists for the good of man.

This volume is an exposition; it is not an argument. The principles of the Gospel, as held by the Church of Jesus Christ of Latter-day Saints, are stated, briefly, simply and without comment, to show the coherence, reasonableness and universality of the gospel philosophy. The authority for many of the statements found in the volume is given in the references included in the appendix. The doctrines herein stated are, however, the common knowledge of the members of the Church. No attempt has been made to correlate the doctrines discussed with current philosophical opinions. Those who are led to study this rational theology in the light of the best knowledge and soundest thought, will enter a fertile field, and will find a surprising harmony between the Gospel and all discovered truth.

The book could not be made larger, were it to serve well the special purpose for which it was written. Therefore, the treatment is brief and many important and interesting subjects are omitted. Moreover, the book had to be completed within a short, set time, and many of the imperfections of the work are the results of the hurried preparation.

Every writer who in this day attempts an exposition of the Gospel must draw heavily upon the clear thoughts of those who, from Joseph Smith to the living workers, have written and spoken in behalf of the truth. I acknowledge, gratefully, my obligation to the makers of "Mormon" literature. Many friends have, also, in various ways, given kindly aid; to them I offer hearty and sincere thanks.

JOHN A. WIDTSOE.

LOGAN, UTAH.

CONTENTS

Rational Theology.

CHAPTER 1.

THE MEANING OF THEOLOGY.

Earth, stars and the vastness of space; yesterday, today and tomorrow, and the endlessly increasing knowledge of the relations of forces, present an illimitable universe of numberless phenomena. Only as a whole, and in general outline, can the human mind understand the universe. In its infinite variety of expressions, it wholly transcends the human mind.

Man in the Universe. In the midst of this complexity, man finds himself. As he progresses from childhood to manhood, and as his slumbering faculties are awakened, he becomes more fully aware of the vastness of his universe and of the futility of hoping to understand it in detail.

Nevertheless, conscious man can not endure confusion. From out the universal mystery he must draw, at least, the general, controlling laws, that proclaim order in the apparent chaos; and, especially is he driven, by his inborn and unalterable nature, to know, if he can, his own place in the system of existing things. Every normal man desires and seeks an understanding of his relation to all other things, and practically every man has worked out for himself, on the basis of his knowledge, some theory which explains, more or less satisfactorily, the mystery of star and earth and man and life. No other quest is followed by man with such vigorous persistence, as is that of establishing an intelligible and satisfactory philosophy of earth-life.

A Man's Religion. The philosophy, or system of thought, adopted to explain man's place in nature determines largely the joy and manner of a man's life. If the philosophy be poor and loose, life will be confused; if rich and firm, life will be clear cut, and if law be made supreme, life will be orderly. Those who have no religion at all become the playthings of unknown forces. Every act of a man's life is influenced by the philosophy of his life. It is the most important product of an individual life, and is the most compelling power in life.

In a broad sense, the philosophy, according to which a man orders his life, may be called that man's religion. It may or may not involve the idea of God or an organized body of believers. If it guides a life, it is that life's religion, whether it leads to weakness or to strength.

Theology Defined. Since all men are placed in the same universe, with approximately the same powers, and under conditions nearly alike, it is possible for each person to establish for himself a religion as above defined, for the guidance of his life. All religions must be organized from the content of the one, and so far as we know, the only universe; and the presumption would be, therefore, that the religions of all men should be the same, in as far at least as men are the same. In fact, however, during the course of human history, many more or less dissimilar religions have been established and accepted. True, most of these religions show close kinship, but the vital differences are often very great. For instance, the religions of men fall naturally into two great classes: those that adopt as their central idea a great governing intelligence and power—a God; and those that refuse to include a God in their system of thought.

A religion which accepts the idea of a God is a theology. The great majority of the religions of men are theologies, for the majority of men believe in some form of personal divine power.

The Gospel. The word gospel is also frequently used, among Christians, to designate the religion of men. The Gospel is a theology which includes the doctrine of the life and mission of Jesus Christ, as the Son of God. Among Christians, the words religion, theology and gospel are freely used in the same sense. It is well, however, to bear in mind the distinction in meaning of the three words. The Christian religion, the Christian theology and the Gospel are equivalent in meaning. In the following pages, the terms are often used interchangeably without the qualifying words. Indeed, the Gospel will be used most frequently, and wherever used, it must be understood to stand for the rational theology discussed in this book.

The Purpose of This Book. This volume is devoted to the exposition of the fundamental principles of a rational theology—a philosophy of life which, because of its complete harmony with all knowledge, should be the one to which all men might give adherence.

CHAPTER 2.

HOW KNOWLEDGE IS GAINED.

Knowledge is the material upon which the reasoning mind of man acts. Just as physical strength can neither be developed nor exercised unless material bodies are at hand, so mental strength can neither be developed nor exercised unless facts or knowledge are in man's possession. The acquisition of knowledge or experience is the first step towards formulating an acceptable religion. It is of interest, therefore, to consider, briefly, the sources of human knowledge.

The Senses. Through eyes, ears, nose, the sense of taste and the complex and poorly understood sense of feeling, man becomes acquainted with the universe. That which is seen by the eyes, heard by the ears, smelled by the nose, tasted by the mouth, or felt by any part of the body, becomes impressed and registered upon the mind, there later to be used. The detailed method by which knowledge is added to man is not understood. The theories that prevail concerning the entrance of knowledge into the human mind need not here be discussed.

It follows that the man who wishes to gain much knowledge must guard his senses from harm, and must sharpen them, so that during the few days of life they may do as much as is possible to help man establish a rational religion for his guidance. The foundation of human knowledge is derived from the direct action of the senses.

The Sixth Sense. Important as are the senses in adding knowledge to man, yet it must be admitted that they recognize without help only a very small part of the universe. Our universe is infinite in its variety of expression—of that man feels certain,— and it could hardly be expected, therefore, that man, who admittedly is yet far from perfection, should be able to know, even with the greatest aid, all of the universe.

The truth that an immeasurable part of the universe lies outside of human experience, is borne in upon every thinking man. In recent times, the developments of science have emphasized this vast region of the unknown. The mystery of electricity, in the telephone and telegraph; the wonder of space, in wireless telegraphy; the marvel of the elements, speak clearly of places and conditions of which we as yet have no clear and accurate conception, and before which the senses of man, unaided, stand helpless.

Nevertheless, glimpses into this unknown region may be had by helps to the senses. By the telescope the far is brought near; by the microscope the small is made large; by the photographic plate unseen light is made visible; by the well tuned coil of wire the wireless message is taken out of space; by the spectroscope, light is broken into its elements, and so on through almost the whole field of human endeavor. Facts that are gathered in such an indirect way are as correctly certain as are those that are sensed directly. The world would lose tremendously should all the truth gathered through aids to the senses be removed.

Man himself, through what may be called, for

want of a better name, the sixth sense, may become
a great aid to his own direct senses. By proper ex-
ertion he may intercept messages from out the directly unknown, as completely as this may be done
by man-made instruments. Throughout history this
power of man has been recognized and usually respected. The experience or knowledge thus gained
should, when properly examined by the mind, be
given an equal place beside that gained directly
through the commoner senses. Prophets, poets,
men of vision and faith, have all builded their
work largely upon this kind of knowledge or in-
ward feeling.

Transmitted Knowledge. The inexhaustible universe and the limited powers of man, make it possible for a person to discover for himself relatively a
very small amount of truth. Much effort may be
saved and more knowledge gained, if each person
learn as much as he may of what has already been
learned, to which he may add the little new discov-
ery that he may make.

This method of obtaining knowledge has been in
vogue since the first day. What the first man
learned, he told to others, and they in turn com-
municated it, with the addition of whatever new
knowledge they had gained. Thus comes the present value of tradition—the spoken record,—and of
books—the written record. Men who desire to build
a safe religion or a safe science, make themselves
familiar with as much as they can of what is already known, instead of attempting to traverse the
known field as original discoverers, and to this
transmitted knowledge, they add whatever in the
course of their pursuit they may discover inde-

pendently. Those who in the present day will accept only what they themselves discover, will make slow progress. To them the treasuries of the greatest age will not be opened.

If, in the course of events, it becomes necessary for God to speak to a man for the benefit of many, it would be contrary to rational thinking that each man for whom the message was given, should directly hear God's voice, unless, indeed, the means of communicating the knowledge become effectually blocked. Such transmitted knowledge is every whit as sound as that acquired by direct communion with nature.

True, the knowledge already possessed by man is so large that it can in nowise be transmitted, in all its details, to one man. The efforts of humanity are directed, therefore, to the devising of general statements, or laws, which embody the meaning of a multitude of facts, while they are yet easily intelligible to the human mind. More and more important will become the repositories of such general principles containing the knowledge of mankind. The Bible, in its various books, presents such great underlying principles of our knowledge relating to several very important phases of earth-life.

The Use of the Reason. Whether knowledge be obtained by any or all of the methods indicated, it should be carefully examined in the light of reason. The only knowledge that will help in the establishment of a satisfactory religion is true knowledge. Truth is the end of the search. False or apparently true knowledge often intrudes itself upon the attention and at times it is so well disguised as to be dangerously deceptive. Man must learn of the uni-

verse, precisely as it is, or he can not sucessfully
find his place in it. A man should therefore use
his reasoning faculty in all matters involving truth,
and especially as concerning his religion.

The Foundation of Rational Theology. The Gospel, or rational theology, is founded on truth, on all
truth, for "truth is knowledge of things as they are,
and as they were, and as they are to come," and
"truth has no end." In building a philosophy of
life a man, therefore, can not say that some truth
must be considered and other truth rejected. Only
on the basis of all truth, that is, all true knowledge,
can his religion be built. Further, the perfection of
his knowledge, that is, the extent of his truth possessions, will determine the value of his religion to
him. Therefore, "it is impossible for a man to be
saved in ignorance," "a man is saved no faster than
he obtains knowledge," and "the glory of God is
intelligence."

CHAPTER 3.

ETERNALISM.

The conceptions necessary for logical thought belong to the Gospel as well as to science, for a satisfactory life philosophy must be based on all knowledge known to man.

All Knowledge, the Basis. The Gospel, as the largest knowledge, must include the knowledge of all sciences. The conceptions of time and space are quite as necessary in theology as in natural science or in any other branch of human thought. The Gospel does not claim, however, possession of ultimate knowledge concerning space or time or other fundamental conceptions. Indeed, man is, ordinarily, allowed to work out for himself the truths of the universe and to organize them into systems of thought which he may follow profitably. Knowledge is given directly by a superior intelligence only when it becomes indispensable. Moreover, there are innumerable phenomena in the universe which can not be explained by the human understanding as at present developed. The distinguishing feature of the Gospel is that it possesses the key to the final philosophy of life. In outline it offers the entire plan of life in the universe; and man may engage for all time to come in the elaboration and development of each department of this great universal plan of human life, without requiring an expansion of the outline. The plan is complete.

Eternal Matter. The saddest feature of man-made religions is their lack of security. One man constructs one theology; another a different one, and men flock hither and thither, accepting the one that appears, for the moment, to be the best, without the deep feeling that the one finally accepted is absolutely the one and only correct system of thought. Yet, this is logically absurd, for a house is either red or not red; a stick is straight or not straight; a man has truth or only the semblance of truth. Two different truths can not be parallel with respect to the same thing. The final philosophy of life must be based on irrevocable truth. That which is true must always remain true, though the applications may change greatly from generation to generation. It is the absence of such fundamental certainties, no doubt, that leads men into a new search for a satisfying religion, or that drives them away from their old theology.

The Gospel of Jesus Christ is obviously a system founded on unvarying certainties. Its doctrines rest on demonstrated truths that lie at the foundation of all sound, acceptable thinking. For instance, as a cornerstone of theology, the Gospel recognizes, in connection with the existence of space and time, the existence of matter. Without matter, the mind of man would have no material on which to act, and the existence of matter becomes, therefore, a fundamental conception of the Gospel. It is the business of man to become acquainted with matter in all of its forms, so far as may be possible, in order to provide a foundation on which the reasoning mind of man may increasingly build its power.

The Gospel holds strictly to the conception of a material universe. Much inconsistency of thought has come from the notion that things occur in a material and an immaterial state. This unthinkable condition has been made the basis of doctrines concerning God and man, which have led to utter confusion of thought. The Gospel accepts the natural view, supported by all human experience, that matter occurs in many forms, some visible to the eye, others invisible, and yet others that may not be sensed by any of the senses of man. In short, there is no such thing as immaterial matter, but some forms of matter are more refined than others. Light, heat, and other similar forces are held by science to be manifestations of a subtle state of matter, beyond the immediate senses of man, which has been called ether. In fact, matter as ordinarily known, and ether, a finer form of matter, are every day conceptions of science. The material universe may appear in a variety of forms; but man recognizes, directly, only that form which is the ordinary matter of our daily lives.

Universal Matter Is Indestructible. Matter is eternal, that is, everlasting. Whether the various forms of matter may be converted one into the other, is not definitely known. Any such conversion would, however, leave the total quantity of matter unchanged. God, the supreme Power, can not conceivably originate matter; he can only organize matter. Neither can he destroy matter. God is the Master, who, because of his great knowledge, knows how to use the elements, already existing, for the building of whatever he may have in mind. The doctrine that God made the earth or man from nothing becomes, therefore, an absurdity. The doctrine of the indestructibility of matter makes possible much theological reasoning that would be impossible without this doctrine.

The nature of matter is not, in and of itself, a subject of deep concern in practical religion. By the slow, laborious methods of man's search for truth, the nature of matter will gradually be revealed. Whether it shall be found to be something distinct, or a form of the universal energy, will not be of consequence in the Gospel structure. That matter, whatever it is, is eternal, is, however, a principle of highest theological value, for it furnishes a foundation for correct reasoning.

Eternal Energy. Matter, wherever found and in whatever form, always possesses energy. It is frequently said that matter in motion, only, can impress the human mind. Matter without motion, were it conceivable, could not be recognized by the human mind as at present constituted. Matter is always associated with energy; energy with matter. It is not conceivably possible to separate them. Whether one is a manifestation of the other, so that there is only matter or only energy, or if they are distinct things, we do not know. All sound thought recognizes, however, the existence of energy throughout the universe. Energy appears in many forms, such as heat, light, electricity, magnetism, gravitation, and, according to the Gospel, the many spiritual forces. These various forms of energy seem to be convertible, one into the other, thus indicating the existence of one central force, of which all other forces are manifestations. The question of energy will probably be answered gradually, as the knowledge of man increases.

Of one thing the Gospel, as well as science, is perfectly certain, namely, that the energy in the universe is indestructible. Changed it may be, from heat to light, from light to electricity, from electricity to magnetism, or from any form to any other form of energy, but destroyed it can not be. Like matter, energy had no beginning and can have no end. God, possessing the supreme intelligence of the universe, can use energy in accomplishing his ends, but create it, or destroy it, he cannot. Undiminished, everacting, universal energy will continue through all times.

Universal Intelligence. In one particular, however, the Gospel goes beyond the teachings of modern science. The Gospel teaches that, associated with the universal energy that vivifies universal matter, and possibly identified with it, is universal intelligence, a force which is felt wherever matter and energy are found, which is everywhere. The forces of the universe do not act blindly, but are expressions of a universal intelligence. That a degree of intelligence is possessed by every particle of energized matter cannot be said; nor is it important. The great consideration is that, since intelligence is everywhere present, all the operations of nature, from the simplest to the most complex, are the products of intelligence. We may even conceive that energy is only intelligence, and that matter and intelligence, rather than matter and energy, are the two fundamentals of the universe!

Eternal Intelligence. Throughout the universe are found, in addition to indestructible matter, everlasting energy and universal intelligence pervading space.

"Man was also in the beginning with God." The doctrine that man is an eternal being leads to untold possibilities. Eternal man lived a personal life before the earth-life began, and he continues a personal existence hereafter.

The Eternal Relationship. The phenomena of the universe result from the interaction of matter, energy and intelligence. These fundamental, universal elements are forever acting upon each other to produce the infinite variety of the universe. Nevertheless, space is not filled with disorder; chaos does not prevail. On the contrary, the universe, so far as known, is essentially orderly. This comes from the great law of cause and effect. If energy acts on matter in a given way, a definite effect is obtained. Under like conditions, the same cause will forever give the same effect. Where, therefore, like conditions are permanently operating, like results will always be found. This law lies at the foundation of the orderliness of nature. "There is a law irrevocably decreed in heaven upon which all blessings are predicated, and it is only by obedience to this law that any blessing may be obtained."

An Eternal Plan. The Gospel itself, the so-called plan of salvation, or Great Plan, in obedience to which men guide their earth-lives, is eternal. It is not a temporary or transient thing, made primarily for the handful of men and women on earth, but it is an eternal plan based upon the everlasting relationship of the elements of the universe—a plan which, in some form, is adapted everywhere and forever, for the advancement of personal beings. This must be so, for it leads to a definite end, and in accordance with the law of cause and effect, it must have a universal meaning.

Eternalism. The Gospel is founded on tangible and eternal things and relationships. These eternal realities, no doubt, in their essence, lie beyond the full understanding of man, just as time and space transcend human understanding. This conception. carried far enough, leads to a gospel or life philosophy which is unshakable, because it rests upon eternal certainty. Without certainty, man is, in the great affairs of life, merely the driftwood of existence, moved hither and thither by the wind of doubt

The Gospel may be said to be The Philosophy of Eternalism. The Gospel is immersed in the ocean of eternity.

CHAPTER 4.

THE WILL OF MAN.

The doctrine of the eternal nature of man is most characteristic of the Gospel. It is a doctrine which gives great satisfaction to all who have accepted the Gospel.

The Primeval Condition. All that is really clear to the understanding is that man has existed "from the beginning," and that, from the beginning, he has possessed distinct individuality impossible of confusion with any other individuality among the hosts of intelligent beings. Through endless ages, man has risen by slow degrees to his present state. Possibly, with respect to the coming day, man understands as little as did the spiritual beings with respect to present day conditions.

The Intelligence of Man. To speculate upon the condition of man when conscious life was just dawning is most interesting, but so little is known about that far-off day that such speculation is profitless. Nevertheless, of some things pertaining to the beginning we are fairly certain. The being which later became man, even in the first day possessed intelligence. That is, he was able to become aware of the external universe, to learn, and by adding knowledge to knowledge, to learn more. Then, as now, the universe was filled with matter acted upon by many forces, and an intelligent being in the midst of the interaction of forces and matter, must have become aware, measurably, of what was going on. From the beginning, the ego of man has been a conscious being, saying to itself, "This is I; that is not I. This life is apart from the life of all the rest of the universe."

The Will of Man. In addition to his power to learn and his consciousness of his own existence, the spiritual personality possessed, from "the beginning," the distinguishing characteristic of every intelligent, conscious, thinking being—an independent and individual will. No one attribute so clearly distinguishes man as does the intelligent will or the will to act intelligently. It was by the exercise of their wills that the spirits in the beginning gathered information rapidly or slowly, acquired experiences freely or laboriously. Through the exercise of their wills they grew, or remained passive, or perhaps even retrograded, for with living things motion in any direction is possible.

Naturally, the original spirit, possessing, with all other attributes of intelligence, the power of will, exercised that will upon the contents of the universe. The exercise of the will upon the matter and energy within reach, enabled the intelligent beings, little by little, to acquire power. By the use of his will upon the contents of the universe, man must have become what he now is.

Value of the Will. The above doctrine involves the idea of self-effort. It is only when the will is exercised in a certain direction that the support of other forces may be invited so that progress in that direction may be accelerated. From the beginning, the deliberate use of the will has moved personal beings onward; and in this latest day of our existence, it is the will that moves men into greater lives. Undoubtedly, the will of man will determine the completion of the structure built through all ages into a perfected man.

The Gospel, resting upon eternal, indestructible principles, maintains the living supremacy of the will of man. The culture, training and use of the will, for good or for evil, determine primarily the direction of an individual life.

CHAPTER 5.

THE GREAT LAW.

The innumerable interactions of the matter, energy and intelligences of the universe, must be held together by some great law. This universal law to which all lesser laws contribute, must be of real concern to the man who seeks a true philosophy of life.

Increasing Complexity of the Universe. It has already been said that a universe controlled by intelligence and under the reign of the law of cause and effect cannot be conceived to be in confusion. Man is absolutely certain, if his knowledge is rational, that, whether it be yesterday, today or tomorrow, the same act, under the same conditions, will produce the same result. Under a set of given conditions, a ray of sunshine passed through a glass prism will always be broken into the same spectrum, or a straight stick standing in water will always appear crooked. Whether in the physical, mental or moral world, the law of cause and effect reigns supreme.

Quiescence in the universe can not be conceived, for then there would be no universe. Constant action or movement characterizes the universe. The multiplicity of actions upon each other, of the various forms of matter, energy and intelligence, composing the universe, must cause an equal multiplicity of effects. Moreover, increasing intelligent wills, acting upon matter and energy, must and do produce an increasing series of reactions among the forces of the universe.

Moreover, each new set of effects becomes the cause of still other effects. Thus, in our universe, as we conceive it to be constituted, increasing complexity would seem to be the great resultant law of the operation of universal forces. This is the great law of nature, to which every living thing must conform, if it is to be in harmony with all other things. In a universe controlled by intelligence, it is only natural to find everything within the universe moving along towards one increasing purpose. As new light has come to man, the certainty of this law as a controlling one, has become more and more emphatic.

Man and the Great Law. The law of increasing complexity is fundamental. Since man is constantly being acted upon and acting upon matter and energy, he must himself be brought under the subjection of the great law. That is, under normal conditions, he will increase in complexity. As man observes phenomena and reasons upon them and applies them he grows in knowledge. Where he formerly had one fact to use, he now has many. This is the essence of his complexity. A carpenter with one tool does less and poorer work than does one with a full kit of modern tools. Likewise, man, as he gathers experience, becomes more powerful in using the forces of nature in the accomplishment of his purposes. With this thought in mind the great law becomes a law of increasing power, of progressive mastery over the universe. For that reason, the law expressing the resultant of the activities of universal forces is often called the law of progression.

The degree of man's growth or progression will depend upon the degree his will is exercised, intelligently, upon the things about him. It is even conceivable that by the misuse of will, man may lose some of his acquired powers. In any case, the operation of the will, under normal conditions, adds power to man; and by the use of the intelligent will in a world of matter and energy, the increasingly complex man grows in power and strength towards perfection, in an increasingly interesting world. Those who do not conform to the law of progression are abnormal and do not exert their powers, to the requisite degree, in the right direction.

Nature is inexhaustible in the possible number of inter-relations among matter, energy and intelligence. It follows, therefore, that man will forever be able to add knowledge unto knowledge, power unto power, or progress unto progress. This law of progression is the great law of the universe, without beginning and without end, to which all other laws contribute. By adherence to this law the willing, intelligent beings have risen to their present splendid state of manhood, and by further compliance with this law they will advance to a future Godlike state of perfection. The supreme intelligence and perfected will of the universe, God, has attained His position by an obedient recognition of the conditions of the law of progression.

The law of progression gives hope and purpose to those who accept the Gospel. The feeling of security that comes from the knowledge that the elements of the universe are eternal, is made living by the hope established by the great law that there is purpose in all the operations of the universe. Whatever man may do, whatever his life may bring, provided all his faculties are working actively among the things and forces about him, he is acquiring knowledge, thereby power, and, under the law of progression, he is being moved onward to a more advanced position than he now occupies, in which he may do mightier work. Men, discouraged by their failure to accomplish exactly what they desire, often speak of their lives as purposeless, but it is idle talk, for, in fact, no intelligent life which concerns itself vigorously with the things about it, can be said to be purposeless. Such a life adheres, automatically, to the law of progression, and is therefore moving on to the great destiny of supreme power and accompanying joys. The only purposeless life is the one that does not use its faculties. It matters little what tasks men do in life, if only they do them well and with all their strength. In an infinite universe, one cannot possibly learn all or do all, at once. A beginning must be made somewhere, and corner by corner, department by department, space by space, all will be known and conquered. In the end, all must be explored, and whether one begin in the east or the west cannot matter much. The big concern is to what extent a man offer himsef, mind and body, to his work. Upon that will growth depend.

The Law of Development. The law of progression is then a law of endless development of all the powers of man in the midst of a universe becoming increasingly complex. No more hopeful principle can be incorporated into a philosophy of life.

CHAPTER 6.

GOD AND MAN.

The doctrine of man's pre-existence leads to an understanding of the relationship between God and man, which must lie at the very basis of rational theology.

Why God is God. To determine this relationship between God and man it is necessary to discuss, first, the conditions under which God became God. As already said, God is the supreme intelligent Being in the universe, who has the greatest knowledge and the most perfected will, and who, therefore, possesses infinite power over the forces of the universe. However, if the great law of progression is accepted, God must have been engaged from the beginning, and must now be engaged in progressive development, and, infinite as God is, he must have been less powerful in the past than he is today. While it is folly for man to attempt to unravel in detail the mystery of the past, yet it is only logical to believe that a progressive God has not always possessed his present position.

It is clear also that, as with every other being, the progress of God began with the exercise of his will. In "the beginning" which transcends our understanding, God undoubtedly exercised his will vigorously, and thus gained great experience of the forces lying about him. As knowledge grew into greater knowledge, by the persistent efforts of will, his recognition of universal laws became greater until he attained at last a conquest over the universe, which to our finite understanding seems absolutely complete. We may be certain that, through self-effort, the inherent and innate powers of God have been developed to a God-like degree. Thus, he has become God.

God, the supreme Being of the universe, absolutely transcends the human understanding. His intelligence is as the sum of all other intelligences. There can be no rational discussion of the details of God's life or nature. To him we give the most complete devotion, for to us he is in all respects infinite and perfect. His Godhood, however, was attained by the use of his power in simple obedience to the laws he discovered as he grew in experience.

Many Gods. During the onward march of the Supreme Being, other intelligent beings were likewise engaged, though less vigorously, in acquiring power over the forces of the universe. Among many intelligent beings thus moving onward, there is little probability of any two attaining exactly the same place, at the same time. There is rather the probability of infinite gradation from the lowest to the highest development. Next to God, there may be, therefore, other intelligent beings so nearly approaching his power as to be coequal with him in all things so far as our finite understanding can perceive. These beings may be immeasurably far from God in power, nevertheless immeasureably far above us mortal men of the earth. Such intelligent beings are as Gods to us. Under this definition there may be a great number of intelligent beings who possess to a greater or less degree the quality of Godhood.

The acceptance of the preceding doctrines makes it almost a logical necessity that there are many gods or beings so highly developed that they are as gods, in fact are Gods. This is a fundamental doctrine of the Gospel.

Why Man is Man. It is fairly evident from what has been said why man is man. Man is subject to eternal laws, and in the far-off beginning he must have exercised his will more slowly or not at all; perhaps, even, as laws came to him he ignored or opposed them. As more knowledge and power are attained, growth becomes increasingly more rapid. God, exalted by his glorious intelligence, is moving on into new fields of power with a rapidity of which we can have no conception, whereas man, in a lower stage of development, moves relatively at a snail-like, though increasing pace. Man is, nevertheless, moving on, in eternal progression. "As man is, God once was; as God is, man may become." In short, man is a god in embryo. He comes of a race of gods, and as his eternal growth is continued, he will approach more nearly the point which to us is Godhood, and which is everlasting in its power over the elements of the universe.

God's Help to Man. Self-effort, the conscious operation of will, has moved man onward to his present high degree. However, while all progress is due to self-effort, other beings of power may contribute largely to the ease of man's growth. God, standing alone, cannot conceivably possess the power that may come to him if the hosts of other advancing and increasing workers labor in harmony with him. Therefore, because of his love for his children and his desire to continue in the way of even greater growth, he proceeded to aid others in their onward progress.

. Knowledge may be transmitted from intelligence to intelligence. God offered to the waiting intelligent beings the knowledge that he had already gained, so that they need not traverse that road, but might attack some other phase of universal existence. He devised plans of progression whereby the experiences of one person might be used by an inferior one. Each person should give of his experience to others, so that none should do unnecessary work. In that manner, through the united effort of all, the whole race of progressive beings would receive an added onward impetus.

Man's Help to God. The progress of intelligent beings is a mutual affair. A lone God in the universe cannot find great joy in his power. God, being in harmony with eternal laws, can progress best as the whole universe becomes more complex, or advances. The development of intelligence increases the complexity of the universe, for each active individual may bring new relationships into view, and increases many-fold the body of acquired truth. In that sense, the man who progresses through his increase in knowledge and power, becomes a colaborer with God, and may be said, indeed, to be a help to God. It is a comforting thought, not only that we need God but also that God needs us. True, the need God has of us is relatively small, and the help he gives us is infinitely large, yet the relation exists for the comfort and assurance of man.

God's Attributes. To analyze the supreme intelligence of the universe, the God whom we worship, is a futile attempt, to which men of shallow minds, only, give their time. That which is infinite transcends the human understanding. The Gospel accepts this condition, calmly, knowing that, in the scheme of things, greater truths will come with increased power, until, in the progress of time, we shall understand that which now seems incomprehensible. For that reason, eternal, or everlasting, or infinite things are things understood by God, the supreme and governing Power, but not understood by us. Thus, "eternal punishment is God's punishment; endless punishment is God's punishment." Likewise, everlasting joy or endless blessings are God's joy and God's blessings. Man acknowledges in this manner that all things are relative to God.

Man does not understand God fully, yet an understanding between man and God does exist in that, God in the course of his progression has gone over the road that we are traveling and therefore understands us fully. He understands our difficulties, our hopes, our sorrows, our faults and our follies. God is supreme, and his justice is perfect; his love is unmeasureable and his mercy without end; for his justice and love and mercy are tempered by the memory of his own upward career. God's relation to man is, in a literal sense, that of father to son, for we are of the same race with God. We may rest secure that God's attributes are, with others, those that man possesses, made great and beautiful. He is our Father who knows and understands us.

CHAPTER 7.

MAN IS THAT HE MAY HAVE JOY.

Is the increasing power of man a sufficient reward for the effort and struggle that must accompany progression? This is a question that comes to every student of the Gospel. Power in itself may not be the ideal end, of existence. It becomes necessary, therefore, to determine if there is associated with power, gifts that make worth while the eternal searching out of knowledge in order that greater power may be won.

Consciousness and the Universe. Intelligent spirits have possessed, from the beginning, a consciousness of the world in which they found themselves. They must have been susceptible, from the first, of feeling pleasure and pain, and must have had equivalents of our senses, which, possibly, were keener than those we now possess. When they were placed in opposition to any law of nature, pain or its equivalent undoubtedly resulted exactly as today. When they moved along with law, joy must have been sensed, as today. Intelligent beings can not rejoice in pain, therefore, from the beginning, to avoid pain and to secure joy, they have searched out and obeyed law. The more advanced the intelligence, the greater the number of laws that are understood to which adaptation may be made, and therefore the greater the possibility of joy. The search for increasing power, carried on by all normal beings is then really a search for a greater and more abiding joy. There is no Godliness in pain, except as it is an incident in securing more knowledge. True freedom, which is full joy, is the complete recognition of law and adaptation to it. Bondage comes from ignorance of law or opposition to it.

The Primeval Condition. Man's approach to a fullness of joy is pictured in his revealed history. Through the veil of forgetting we see but dimly our pre-existent condition. The Gospel student does not really concern himself, greatly, with the details of the life before this one; so much needs to be done in this life that he is content with the great outlines of pre-existent life, which may assist him to understand the eternal journey of intelligence. Of the primeval condition of man little is known. He found about him many forces, operating in diverse ways, and to control them, and thus to sense joy, he began to study them. The story of that early day of striving for the greatest goal has not been told to mortal man.

The First Estate. Matter exists, perhaps, in many forms, but may be classified, as the ponderable matter of earth, known directly through the senses, and, as the imponderable matter which cannot be sensed directly by man. This second class, often called spirit matter, is perhaps most important, for it is not unlikely that from it are derived all other forms of matter.

It was of first importance that the intelligent beings aiming at the conquest of the universe, should learn to understand, thoroughly, the properties of universal matter, in all of its forms. As nearly as can be learned, the efforts of man were first devoted to education in the properties of spirit matter. We were begotten spirits by God, who thus became our Father, and we are his sons and daughters. Our career in the spirit world is often spoken of as man's first estate.

How long man remained in the first estate, is not known. Undoubtedly, however, it was long enough to enable him to become thoroughly familiar with the manifestations of all forms of spirit substance. Only when education in this division of the universe was completed were we permitted to enter the next estate.

The Second Estate. The kind of matter characteristic of this earth and the so-called material universe, also forms an important part of the universe. No spirit can acquire real mastery over the universe until this form of matter is so thoroughly understood as to be used and governed. The next step in the education of these intelligent beings was therefore to teach them familiarity with gross matter. Consequently, the spirits passed out of the spirit world, and were born into the world of earthly things, the world we now occupy, as men and woenm clothed upon by a body consisting of gross matter, so that intimate familiarity with the nature and possibilities of gross matter might be acquired. This is called the second estate of man.

The business of man is to become so thoroughly acquainted with earth conditions, that through the possession of an earthly body, he may go on, forever,

The Third Estate. We pass out of this, but reappear in another world, for a brief time separated from our earth-won body, but finally possessing bodies of both kinds of universal matter. In this estate, both the spirit matter and the grosser matter composing our final bodies are represented by their essences, and therefore permit perfect freedom and ease of movement and thought. These celestial bodies, as they are called, connect the intelligence with all parts of the universe, and become mighty helps in the endless search for truth. This is the third estate of man.

Such then are the three estates, and as far as known, all the estates of man.

Whether the outline, as here presented, in its details, is precise or not, matters little. The essential thing is that man has to undergo experience upon experience, to attain the desired mastery of the external universe; and that we, of this earth, are passing through an estate designed wholly for our further education.

Everlasting Joy. It follows that, in each estate, with each onward step, a profounder knowledge of the laws of nature is attained. When conscious, active wills are thus at work, the new knowledge makes possible a more perfect adaptation of man to law. The more completely law is obeyed the greater the consciousness of perfect joy. Throughout eternal life, increasing knowledge is attained, and with increasing knowledge comes the greater adaptation to law, and in the end an increasingly greater joy. Therefore it is that eternal life is the greatest gift of God, and that the plan of salvation is priceless.

CHAPTER 8.

MAN'S FREE AGENCY.

The question of the rights of each intelligent being as pertaining to himself and to all others must always have been and must always remain a chief one.

In the Beginning. In each intelligent being has resided, from the beginning, an individual and distinct will, which, of itself, has been acting in some degree upon the external universe. Each being, with its developing will, has learned more and more of natural forces and of the methods of controlling them. Each has striven to adapt his knowledge of surrounding forces to his own particular needs or desires. Clearly, since many wills have been so en-engaged, it might easily occur that different wills might use acquired knowledge in different ways to suit their different desires. It is easily conceivable, therefore, that one will might attempt so to control the surrounding forces as to give itself joy, yet to affect another will adversely. In general, whatever is desirable for one is desirable for all, since all spirits are cast in the same mold and have the same derivation. Nevertheless, when individuality is assumed, it is equally clear that there is always a possibility of one will crossing another to the detriment of one or possibly both.

The universal plan may follow its developing path, unhindered, only when all the intelligent beings within it labor harmoniously together for the upbuilding of each and all. The only solution for the

—

problem of the possible conflicts resulting from the activities of a great number of beings is an agreement among them relating to the general good.   Laws established for the community of beings must be obeyed as rigidly as those found in external nature.   Each may act freely and to his full power in any desired way so long as the general laws respecting the freedom of all others are not violated.   The right of an individual can never transcend the rights of the community.

The Council in Heaven. A dim though wonderfully attractive picture has come down of an event in the spiritual estate of man, the first estate, that deals directly with the great question of the one and the many, the individual and the community.

There had been born, in time, a family of spirits, the innumerable destined hosts of earth, who, at length, seemed fitted for further education in another field.   God, the Father of these spirits, saw that they were ready for further light, and came down among them, to discuss their future.   As the Supreme Being, God had in mind a plan, the Great Plan, whereby each spirit could enter upon his second estate and become acquainted with the properties of gross matter.   However, as each intelligent spirit possessed a free and untrammeled will which must be respected, God called together the spirits in question, and presented the plan for their approval.

In the Great Council then held, of which a dim and distant picture only has been left, the great question was with respect to man's free agency. The essence of the proposed plan was that the

4

spirits, forgetting temporarily their sojourn in their spirit home should be given a body of grosser matter, and should be subject to this form of universal matter, and even be brought into a temporal death. To bring an eternal, free spirit under the bondage of matter and forgetfulness, it was necessary for some one to begin the work by, figuratively speaking, breaking a law, so that the race might be brought under the subjection of death. This may be likened, roughly, to the deliberate breaking, for purposes of repair or extension, of a wire carrying power to light a city. Someone had to divert the current of eternal existence, and thus temporarily bring man's earthly body under the subjection of gross matter.   Adam, the first man, was chosen to do this work.   By the deliberate breaking of a spiritual law, he placed himself under the ban of earthly death and transmitted to all his posterity the subjection to death. This was the so-called "sin of Adam." To obtain or give greater joys, smaller pains may often have to be endured.

The Need of a Savior. The purpose of the earth career was, however, two-fold, to learn to understand gross matter, and to acquire a body made of the essence of such matter. The bodies laid in the grave must, therefore, be raised again.   As the spirits, by their own act had not brought upon themselves death, so by their own act they should not conquer it. It was necessary, therefore, that someone, in time, should reunite the broken wires and re-establish the flow of eternal life, and thus to conquer death. For this work Jesus Christ was chosen. Jesus actually came on earth, lived and taught the ancient Gospel again to the children of

men, and in time suffered death so that the act of
Adam might be atoned for. By this work, the purpose of the earth-life was completed, and thus Jesus
Christ became the central figure in the plan of salvation.

Why death, so-called, should be necessary for us
to achieve an intimate knowledge of matter, and
why Jesus should die to permit the current of eternal
life to flow freely between the earthly body and the
eternal spirit, are not fully known. Through
Adam man was brought on earth, subject to death;
through Jesus, the Christ, he was lifted out of death
to continue an eternal life in association with the
earth-acquired body.

Man's Part in the Great Plan. In this great gathering in the heavens many questions arose. By
Adam man was to come on earth; by Jesus he was
to be resurrected. In both of these great acts, man
had no part, beyond permitting himself to be acted
upon. In the plan, what was to be man's part?

Lucifer, a great leader in the Council, proposed
that, since others were acting for man in bringing
him on and taking him away from the earth, it was
not necessary for man, during his earth-career, to
exercise his own will. Lucifer proposed that, in
spite of himself, his will, his desires and his individuality, man should be placed on earth, and be
taken from it, and without effort, be filled with a
knowledge of earth conditions. All men should be
forced into salvation. Jesus Christ, who became
the Savior of men, objected to this change in
God's plan, as it interfered with the essential
right of intelligent beings to act for themselves.
Jesus insisted that, as without will there can be no

growth, man, placed on earth through the agency of Adam and resurrected and brought into a full life through the agency of Jesus, should retain, during his earth-career, his full free agency. Though he might walk in forgetfulness of the past, and have no visions of the future, he would yet be allowed a free and untrammeled agency as he walked in the clearness of the earth's day. While upon earth he might learn much or little, might accept a law or reject it, just as he had been privileged to do in all the days that had gone before.

These two views regarding man's part in the plan led, we are told, to a great difference of opinion among the spirits. Naturally, the first proposition appealed to many, for it is the easy way of obtaining victory, if victory it may be called. The other way seems always somewhat hard and bitter, though in the end the joy obtained surpasses that attained without effort. Lucifer, who led the fight for the first method, could not agree to the original plan which was finally accepted; and so, in that great, dim day, many of the spirits followed Lucifer, and have not yet entered upon their earth-careers, but are independently and in opposition to God's will, following paths that are not leading them onward. The majority accepted God's law, as championed by the Son, though it is said that many weak and fearful spirits remained neutral, daring neither to accept nor to reject either proposition. The hosts who accepted the plan of God, girded themselves with the necessary strength to begin the pilgrimage, ending in an earthly death, but reaching, through the resurrection, into an eternal life of exceedingly great progress.

Free Agency. On the earth, as elsewhere, then, the free agency of man, as expressed in the individual will, is supreme. Though our environment is that of gross matter, and though we dwell in forgetfulness of the past, our free agency is as vigorous as ever. However, the free agency of man cannot transcend the plan which all of us of earth accepted, together, in the day of the Great Council. Man's will is always circumscribed by great laws that are self-existent or that are formulated or may be formulated for the benefit of the race. The many must devise laws whereby individual and community progress are simultaneous. It is the full right of the individual to exercise his will in any way that does not interfere with the laws made for the many; and, under proper conditions, the laws for the many are of equal value to the individual. Under the law we are free.

CHAPTER 9.

THE GREAT PLAN.

The plan proposed by God for the government of the spirits who entered upon their earth careers is revealed only so far as it is necessary for the guidance of man. We may remain certain that the Great Plan is based upon eternal laws that always have been and always will be operative. Matters pertaining to man's earth-life are matters of eternal interest; and the laws formulated for the guidance of man on earth must be laws which in some form are fundamental for the guidance of man in any place and at all times. Nothing is temporary or transient about the Plan itself, for it rests on eternal foundations.

Forgetfulness. A condition of the Plan seems to be that the spirits, transferred to this earth, shall remain on earth in forgetfulness of an earlier existence. As in a dream, in moments of deep spiritual fervor, do we occasionally seem to recall our pre-existent life. A veil has been drawn over the past; and, without the aid of memory, man fights his battle with the world of gross matter. This forgetfulness seems reasonable. The spirit of man accepted the earth-plan in detail, and if he remembered every step that led to this acceptance, and every detail of the Plan itself, there would not be much reason for the exercise of will in adhering to it. Left as he is, with little memory to steady him, he must exercise all his power, to compel surrounding forces to serve him in searching out the past and in prophesying for the future. By such vigorous exercise of his will he develops a more intimate acquaintanceship with the things of the earth.

Subject to Earth Conditions. Intimacy with the conditions of earth, alone, will give a man final knowledge of them. Such information can not be obtained second hand nor by casual or superficial acquaintanceship. For that reason, probably, man has been brought so completely under the subjection of gross matter, that he has no power over it beyond that which he gains as he obtains knowledge of it. Hence, on this earth, stripped of all power, and left, as it were, helpless in the midst of contending universal forces, man must search out the nature of the things about him and determine their laws before he acquires power over nature and thereby brings himself into a condition of joy. In the face of the impending change called death, man is possibly more determined to acquire the power that will lift him from the grave and give him an eternal association with all the elements of the universe, including his earthly body.

Laws to be Obeyed To enter into the fullness of progressive joy, a man must, as has been said, naturally subject himself to the laws of the universe. In God's Plan for life on earth, is a system of laws, representing eternal realities, to which man must conform. Such a law, for instance, is faith, which, in its simple universal meaning, is man's certainty that in the universe is found everything he may desire for his upbuilding and advancement, and that the eternal relations of universal forces will prevail for his good.   Another such fundamental law to which man must conform, is that of repentance, which in its larger sense, is merely faith made active. Passive faith can do little for man's advancement. Yet another such law is that of baptism, which is essentially obedience to existing laws.' And still another such law is that of the gift of the Holy Ghost, which perhaps means that a man may place himself in touch with the whole of the universe and to draw knowledge from it, including the beings of superior intelligence that it contains. These and other laws are given as guides for man.   They sharpen his free agency ; develop his habits of obedience to law, and establish for him communication with God.   Moreover, a plan formulated by an intelligent Being must be composed of laws, for even the infinite relationships of matter and energy fall naturally into groups of invariable laws. The laws of the Plan, like those above stated, are logical necessities, if the earth-plan is at all accepted.

An Organization.   It follows of necessity that if there is a plan, there must also be an organization. The plan is not for one alone, but for many. All must be served and blessed by the Great Plan. Those, therefore, who subject themselves to the earth-plan with its laws, must needs group themselves so that the laws may be operative for all.   A person may be able to serve in the advancement of the whole race of man, only when there is a unity of purpose and effect, which can be secured only by organization. The question of organization involves those of priesthood, authority, and others, later to be discussed.

All to Accept the Plan.   The earth-plan, fully

completed, must be accepted or definitely rejected by all the spirits who have appeared on earth in conformity with their vote in the Great Council. That is fundamental. Those who enter upon their earth-careers may accept or reject the Gospel; but, since the full success of the Plan is based upon the advancement of all the spirits, it becomes necessary to use every possible effort to secure for the Plan a recognition of all those who accepted it in the spirit world, and who, therefore, entered upon the pilgrimage of earth. God's purpose in the Plan will be incomplete so long as one soul remains unconverted.

Life on earth deals directly with gross matter and the forces pertaining to it. The laws formulated for the guidance of man, are especially devised for earth conditions, and belong to the earth. For instance, baptism, the symbol of obedience to God and acceptance of his love, is not necessarily an ordinance that belongs elsewhere than on earth. More probably, water baptism is essentially an ordinance of and for this earth. It is unlikely that water baptism is practiced in a future estate. If it be true, then all who enter upon the earth-career, and who desire at the years of discretion the perfected joy derived from the Gospel, must have baptism on this earth. Should some of the spirits refuse, while on earth, to accept the Gospel, or fail to hear it, baptism, belonging to the earth, must be done for them, vicariously, on earth, so that they, having had the work done for them here, may accept or reject the ordinance in their life beyond the grave. This is the motive of the work for the dead. The earth ordinances must be done by or for every soul born upon the earth so that the earth experience may not be in vain, should the Gospel be accepted in the remotest day of eternity. This view becomes more important when it is recalled that ordinances of the earth, belonging primarily to the earth, stand for vast, eternal realities, indispensable to man's progress.

When the simple ordinances of the Gospel, as pertaining to the earth, have been done for the dead, then may the dead be judged as of the earth, and may receive the blessings of the obedient who conform to law.

The Meaning of the Earth Plan. The earth-plan, plan of salvation, or Great Plan, for the guidance of the spirits placed on earth, may perhaps be more clearly understood if it is compared to the great chart in the captain's cabin by which the vessel is steered. Life on earth is as the large and angry ocean. The chances of shipwreck and of being driven out of the set course, are many. If, however, the ocean is well charted, the mariners can better avoid the sunken reefs, and the dangerous places, and after the storm can more readily return to the course so that the destined port may be entered with a good bill of health. The Gospel is such a chart, on which the journey is outlined, showing the dangers of the journey, the havens of rest and the final destination. If a man accept the chart, and use it in his life's career, he will find the voyage pleasant and his arrival secure, and his life will be as that of one cast in pleasant places.

The Beginning of the Earth Work

CHAPTER 10.

THE COMING OF MAN.

The decision arrived at in the Great Council was promptly carried out by those to whom the authority to do so was confided.

Making of the Earth. The first step, in carrying out the Great Plan, was to secure a place on which the desired experience might be gained. To accomplish this, the earth was made from materials, found in the universe, which, by the intelligent power of God, were collected and organized into the earth. The earth was not made from nothing, nor by the fiat of God, except as his will and words determined that the work should be undertaken. In the clumsy way of man, by adding stone to stone or material to material, the earth was not made; rather, great forces, existing in the universe, and set into ceaseless operation by the directing intelligence of God, assembled and brought into place the materials constituting the earth, until, in the course of long periods of time, this sphere was fitted for the abode of man. In the making of the earth, as in all other matters pertaining to the destiny of man, the work was done in complete and orderly harmony with the existing laws of the universe. The Mosaic six days represent successive stages in the earth's construction, each measured by ages of time. The forces of nature act steadily but slowly in the 'accomplishment of great works.

The Builders. The creation of the earth, the details of which are not known, must have been marvelously and intensely appealing in its interest to the intelligent beings who, because of their exalted knowledge, had the necessary power over the elements and forces of the universe to accomplish the forming of an earth. Three great intelligent Beings were in supreme authority in the building of the earth, namely, God, the Father, his Son, Jehovah, who became the Christ, and Michael, who became the first man, Adam. These three beings were naturally the ones concerned in the making of an earth for the sojourn of the spirits, for it was through the agency of God, the Father, that the spiritual bodies were started on the road of eternal progression; it was about the mission of Jehovah, the Son of God, that the differences of opinion raged in the Great Council, and, finally, it was Adam, or Michael, who was appointed to be the one to come upon the earth, and there to subject himself to death, so that the procreation of spirits in earthly tabernacles, might be started. These three beings, who are so vitally concerned in the destinies of the human race, had charge of the making of an earth which should be a suitable and a pleasant habitation for the earth-clad spirits.

The Coming of Man The earth at last was finished. Adam, the first man, and his wife, Eve, then appeared on earth. The statement that man was made from the dust of the earth is merely figurative, and means that he was made of universal materials, as is the earth. Likewise, the statement that God breathed into man the breath of life is only a figure of the existence of the spirit within the body. The exact process whereby man was placed upon earth is not known with certainty, nor is it vital to a clear understanding of the plan of salvation. We may rest assured that the first man and the first woman were eternal beings, who subjected themselves to life on this earth, so that the process of clothing eternal spirits with mortal bodies might begin on the earth. Adam and Eve, in view of the great sacrifices they made to make the Great Plan a reality, are the great hero and heroine of human history.

The "Fall." Biblical lore and traditions among all of the races of man, tell of the "fall" of the first parents from the grace of God. An event called the fall did occur, but it was a necessary part of the Great Plan. Adam and Eve were eternal beings, and were not under the ban of mortal death. Subject to death they must become, however, if their posterity should inherit corruptible bodies. The fall then was simply a deliberate use of a law, by which act Adam and Eve became mortal, and could beget mortal children. The exact nature of this event or the exact manner in which the law was used is not understood. The Bible account is, undoubtedly, only figurative. There was no essential sin in the fall, except that the violation of any law, whether deliberately or otherwise, is always followed by an effect. The "fall" of Adam and Eve was necessary, for without it, there would have been no begetting on the earth of spirits with mortal bodies, and the Plan proposed and confirmed in the Great Council would have remained inoperative. "Adam fell that man might be."

The First Blessing The curse, so-called, pronounced by God upon Adam as he went out of the

Garden of Eden, that in the sweat of his brow he should earn his bread, is possibly the greatest of all human blessings, and it is a simple extension of a great eternal law. From the beginning of the dim past, when man slumbered with only a feeble thought of his possible vast future, the great law of his progress has been that only personal effort can achieve desirable things. The price to be paid for advancement is vigorous self-effort. The active will precedes every step of progress. To exercise the will means labor, which may well be represented by "the sweat of the brow." The so-called curse, however, carries with it the magnificent promise that man, by the exercise of his powers, may subdue the earth, and make it serve all his needs. In a universe controlled and directed by the intelligent God, there can be no question but that, ultimately, the intelligent will shall control for its own use not only the things of this earth but all the forces of the universe. The subjection to which the earth will be brought depends entirely upon the degree to which man exercises his will, that is, the degree to which he accepts the benefits of the first blessing.

The Garden of Eden. The first days on earth of the first man and the first woman are of intense interest to every student of the subject, and it is to be regretted that so little knowledge of those early times has survived the vicissitudes of time. In the Garden God walked with man and taught him the living truth. According to the Prophet Joseph Smith, the Garden of Eden, the first home of Adam and Eve, was located near the city known as Independence, Missouri. To the north and east of Independence, some scores of miles, is probably the place where Adam dwelt after he had been driven out of the Garden. The State of Missouri, and the country around it, is, therefore, of tremendous interest to those who accept the Gospel as restored in the latter days.

A Wise Beginning. In all matters pertaining to the beginning of man's earth career, it may be observed that proper preparations have been made. There has been no blind destiny working out unknown purposes; instead, intelligent forces have provided for man from beginning to end, so that the whole scheme of man's life, here and hereafter, is one of order and system.

CHAPTER 11.

THE COURSE OF THE GOSPEL ON EARTH.

The Great Plan provided that man should come upon earth with the memory of his past taken from him, so that, beginning his earth-life as a child, he might repeat on earth the efforts that earned for him progress in the pre-existent life. Even Adam and Eve forgot the details of their previous lives, for it was necessary that all be under the same law, and that no improper strength be derived, by anyone, from the pre-existent experiences.

Adam Hears the Gospel. The only rational thing that could be done to spirits so placed on earth was to teach them fully the story of man's origin and destiny and the meaning and duties of the earth-life. The plea of ignorance would not then be valid. Consequently, soon after the first parents had been driven out of the Garden of Eden, an angel appeared and taught Adam the story of man from the first to the last day. The plan of salvation, including the atoning sacrifice of Jesus, the organized Church, the purpose and powers of the priesthood and the rights and duties of man upon earth, whether within or without the Church, was fully unfolded. Adam, the first earth-pupil of God, was taught, as his first lesson, the great philosophy overshadowing the existence of man. When Adam had been taught all this, and had accepted the truth, he was baptized, even as men are baptized today, and he entered into all the other ordinances of the Gospel and was given full authority through the Priesthood conferred upon him to officiate in God's name in all matters pertaining, under the Great Plan, to the welfare of man.

The First Dispensation. As children and children's children came to Adam he taught them carefully all that had been taught him, so that the knowledge of the law might remain upon the earth. The ordinances of the Gospel were practiced, the righteous were organized into the Church, even as today, and the authority of the Priesthood was transmitted by Adam to his children, and by them to their children, so that the precious gift might not be lost. In those days the Church was probably fully organized, according to the patriarchal order; at least in the days of Enoch, the seventh from Adam, it seems quite clear that the Church was established with all of its essential parts. The activity in behalf of the Gospel which began with Adam and continued until Noah, at the time of the great flood, is ordinarily known as the first dispensation of the Gospel.

The First Apostasy. From the beginning of his earth-career, Adam retained his free agency. God, directly or through agents, might teach and command, but Adam, a free agent, had the right to accept or reject as seemed him best. Adam's children, likewise, though taught by the patriarch of the race of the way of righteousness, could accept or reject for themselves whatever was taught them. Free agency was with man in that early day as it is now.

The descendants of Adam soon began to exercise their free agency, some for, and many against, the Great Plan. Cain exercised his free agency in the murder of Abel. As time went on, large numbers departed from the truth concerning man's place in the universe as taught by Adam, and refused to accept the Gospel. Concurrently with the establishment of the Church in the first dispensation there was, therefore, a first great apostasy. It is ever so, it has ever been so, and will ever be so, that in a world of intelligent beings, possessing free agency, some will accept and some will reject the truth. No doubt, in the process of time, truth will triumph, and all may be brought to understand the will of God, but the conquest is attended by many temporary departures from the truth. Nevertheless, Adam and those who remained true to his teachings, continued, faithfully, to teach to others the eternal truth, so that they might perchance be made to return to the great truth which they had so lightly cast aside.   ·

The Later Dispensations. The first apostasy culminated in the flood, which was sent because of the violence of the first apostasy and the corruption of men. As far as known, only Noah and his immediate family were preserved. In them, however, was represented all the blood of the world. To the new race Noah explained fully that the flood was due, entirely, to the wicked hardness of the hearts of the people, and their refusal to accept eternal truth or to respect the authority of God, and that it was necessary, should calamity be avoided, to live in accordance with the Great Plan. To them all, the Gospel was taught in its purity. Nevertheless, it was only a short time before apostasy again occurred among many. The free agency of man can not be curbed. Yet, probably, there has not been, since the flood, such utter corruption as prevailed during the first apostasy.

From the days of the flood, God or his messengers have appeared on earth, at various times, to restore the truth or to keep it alive in the hearts of the faithful, so that man might possess a full knowledge of the Gospel and that the earth might never need to be without the story of the Great Plan and the authority of the Priesthood. For instance, Melchizedek, the high priest, possessed a full measure of the authority of the holy priesthood. To Abraham, God and his angels appeared, and endowed him with the authority of God. So on, down the course of time, there are numerous instances of the appearance of God to men to help the children of men to a perfect understanding of the great truths that must be understood and obeyed, if men are to continue in their progressive development. It is not known how many men and women at various times have received such visitations, but it is probable that hosts of men and women at various times, even when the Church has not been organized, have received and used the truth of life as embodied in the Great Plan.

The Dispensation of the Meridian of Time. In the course of human history and in accordance with the Great Plan, Jesus the Son of God, appeared on earth, to atone for the act of Adam and Eve, who "fell" that men might be. This is called the dispensation of the meridian of time. Jesus did live on earth, and gave his life so that mortal bodies may rise from the grave and pass into an eternal existence, beyond the reach of corruption. During the sojourn of Jesus on earth, he devoted himself to a restatement of the Gospel, including the story of the past and the present and the hope of the future. At no time since the days of Adam, had the Gospel been so fully taught and made so simply clear to the understanding as in the days of Jesus. Under the teachings of the Savior, the Church was re-established in order and completeness.

The Great Apostasy. After the ascension of Jesus, the Church remained, for some time, fully organized. Thousands flocked to it, and the people lived in accordance with the doctrines taught by the Savior. Soon, however, history repeated itself. In the right of their free agency, men refused, in many cases, to obey the laws and ordinances of the Gospel, and more often changed them to suit their own convenience. Such departures from the truth became more numerous and more flagrant as time wore on, until error permeated the whole Church. At last, about six hundred years after Christ, the Gospel laws and ordinances had become so completely warped that it was as if the Church had departed from the earth. The authority of the Priesthood no longer remained with the Church. This was the great apostasy. From that time, complete darkness reigned for many centuries. In those days, however, many honest men could see that the truth was not upon the earth, and hoped that the simple principles of the Gospel might again be correctly practiced by man. Among such men were Luther and many others, who used their best endeavors to show the people that error ruled. At last many were awakened, and the days of the Reformation be- began. The Reformation was a period of preparation for the last restoration of the Gospel on earth.

Many years were required before the darkness of centuries could be lifted from the souls of men.

The Restoration. Finally, as men broke through the darkness, as intelligence became diffused among all men, and as liberality of thought grew and became respected, the world was ready for the eternal truth. Again the Gospel was restored with the authority of the Priesthood and the organization of the Church. On an early spring day, in the year 1820, in the woods of western New York, God the Father, and God the Son, appeared to a fourteen-year-old boy named Joseph Smith, who had faithfully asked for divine help. Through the instrumentality of this boy, guided constantly by God, the Church was re-established, the authority of the Priesthood again conferred upon many men, and a fulness of knowledge pertaining to man's place in the universe offered to all who would listen. In time the Church was organized precisely as was the primitive Church, and more fully than at any other time in the history of the world. This was the great restoration.

The Vital Facts. The Gospel was fully taught to the first man, who in turn taught it to others. The Church was organized from the beginning. As apostasy dimmed men's knowledge of the Gospel and undermined the Church, the full truth was repeatedly restored. At least four times has a complete statement of the Great Plan been made to the people of the earth—at the time of Adam, of Noah, of Jesus Christ and of Joseph Smith. Consequently, the Gospel has been on the earth and within the reach of men practically during the whole course of the earth's history. The fundamental truths of the

Great Plan were taught to Father Adam and since that time have been scattered broadcast over the earth. This wide dissemination of the truth, in all ages, explains the fact that practically every life philosophy proposed by man contains some of the truths of the Gospel. In every system of theology and in every sect there is a certain measure of truth, for all have drawn from the one fountain. All, no doubt, seek for truth, and believe that they have found it; but, in fact, they have only fragments, picked up here and there and worked into a system. The full truth must encompass the complete philosophy of man and the universe, including the authority to act for God in the working out of the Plan. Those who thus accept the whole Plan, constitute the Church of Christ. In the churches of the world there is much of truth and consequently none is wholly wrong, though at times the truth has been so warped that it appears worse than untruth. In the matter of full truth, and of authority, however, do the Church and its imitators differ absolutely. There can be no duplicate set of truth, and no double seat of authority.

It is clear that free agency, for which the heavenly battle was waged, is in full operation upon the earth. At first sight it may seem that Lucifer's plan would have been best, for by it all men, in spite of themselves, would have been given the earth-experience and kept in the righteous path that leads to salvation. Yet, the origin of man, and the doctrine that he can advance only by self-effort, make it unthinkable that he should allow himself to be, as it were, blindfolded and then compellingly directed by some greater power. Men are directed, no doubt, by beings of higher intelligence, but in that directing our wills must be allowed to play their part. There can be no real satisfaction, if it were possible, in advancement which has been forced upon man Lucifer's plan was impossible.

It must also be remembered, that men are not necessarily evil because they do not accept the Gospel. Some find it impossible to understand the truth because their hearts are so set upon other things, and others have been led by their free agency in one direction, whereas the Gospel would lead them in another. Neverthless, though men are not evil because they refuse to accept the Gospel, they retard themselves of necessity, when they fail to obey the law; and thereby they invite upon themselves the punishment that comes without fail to all who are not in full harmony with the great, controlling universal laws.

Man and God.

CHAPTER 12.

THE GODS OF THIS EARTH.

The conception of a universe directed by a God of intelligence can not include a God of mystery. In mystery there is only confusion. It does not follow that because he is not mysterious he is fully comprehended. In our general conception of God, his origin, his destiny, and his relation to us, we understand him clearly; but, in the details of his organization, powers and knowledge he transcends our understanding. Intelligent man dwelling in a universe containing many superior intelligent beings will often find need of the help that higher intelligence only can give. Earth-bound as we are, we need a close acquaintance with the God who shapes the destinies of men. The better God is known, the better may the eternal truths we learn be applied in our daily lives.

The Order of Gods. God has had no beginning and will have no end. From the first, by the exercise of his will, he has constantly acquired new knowledge and thereby new power. Because of the wisdom which he has gained, and the love thereby begotten for the unnumbered hosts of striving intelligent beings, he formulated the plan which will lead them readily and correctly in the way of continued progression. In so far as man accepts the plan of salvation he is being educated by God, to become even as God is. God and man are of the same race, differing only in their degrees of advancement.

True, to our finite minds, God is infinitely beyond our stage of progress. Nevertheless, man is of the order of Gods, else he cannot know God.

Plurality of Gods Since innumerable intelligent beings are moving onward in development, there must be some in almost every conceivable stage of development. If intelligent beings, far transcending the understanding of man, be called Gods, there must be many Gods. God, angel and similar terms denote merely intelligent beings of varying degree of development. The thought, however, that there is a plurality of gods and other beings of varying grades, is a thought of fundamental truth, which may be applied in every-day life, for it gives the assurance that it is possible for all, by self-effort and by gradual steps, to attain the highest conceivable power.

A division of labor is necessary among men on earth, and it is only reasonable that a similar division of labor may exist in all intelligent systems. The conception of a community of men may be applied to the community of heavenly beings. In the community of men, different men have different duties; so, perhaps, on an exalted scale, the gods are organized with a perfected division of labor.

God, the Father. God, the Father, the greatest God concerned in our progression, is the supreme God. He is the Father of our spirits. He is the being of highest intelligence with whom we deal. To our senses and understanding he is as perfection. In his fulness he can not be fathomed by the human mind, and it is, indeed, useless for man to attempt to define in detail the great intelligent beings of the universe.

God, the Father, the supreme God, has gone through every phase of the Great Plan, which we are working out. Therefore, he has had our experiences or their equivalents, and understands from his own experience the difficulties of our journey. His love for us is an understanding love. Our earth troubles we may lay fully before him, knowing that he understands how human hearts are touched by the tribulations and the joys of life.

God, the Father, the supreme God of whom we have knowledge, is the greatest intelligence in the infinite universe, since he is infinite in all matters pertaining to us and transcends wholly our understanding in his power and wisdom. We know no greater God than the omniscient, omnipotent Father.

God, the Son. With the Father is associated his only begotten Son on earth, Jesus Christ, who came on earth and submitted himself to a painful and ignoble death so that all men might be raised from the grave with the body of flesh and bones made indestructible and everlasting. Because of the central position occupied by Jesus in the Great Plan, he is essentially the God of this earth. He, also, is beyond our understanding, he sits on the right hand of the Father, and is one with the Father in all that pertains to the welfare of the human race. To us he is perfect, possessing all the attributes of the Father. Whether he is as far advanced as the Father is an idle question, since he surpasses our understanding. In all matters pertaining to the earth, the Son is the agent of the Father. Through him the will of the Father pertaining to this earth is given. All our communications with the Father are made in the name of the Son, so that they may be

properly authorized. This is in simple accord with
the order that prevails in the heavens and that
should prevail everywhere on earth.

God, the Holy Ghost. The Father and the Son
and the Holy Ghost constitute the Godhead, or
Trinity of Gods, guiding the destinies of men on
earth. God, the Holy Ghost, is a personage of
spirit, who possesses special functions which have
not yet been clearly revealed. We know that this
member of the Godhead is a knowledge-giver and
an inspirer of all that is great and noble and desirable, and that his functions in the Godhead are indispensable to the welfare of man.

Other Beings Many other intelligent beings,
superior to us, no doubt take part in the work of
man on earth. There are angels and spirits who no
doubt have assigned to them the care of the men
and women who walk upon the earth. Man is not
alone; he walks in the midst of such heavenly com-
pany, from whom he may expect help if he seek it
strongly. A plan for the schooling of intelligent
spirits, walking in semi-darkness through the ac-
quiescence of beings of higher intelligence, must of
a certainty include such continuous though invisible help.

Sex Among the Gods. Sex, which is indispensable
on this earth for the perpetuation of the human race,
is an eternal quality which has its equivalent everywhere. It is indestructible. The relationship between men and women is eternal and must continue
eternally. In accordance with the Gospel philosophy
there are males and females in heaven. Since we
have a Father who is our God, we must also have a

mother, who possesses the attributes of Godhood. This simply carries onward the logic of things earthly, and conforms with the doctrine that whatever is on this earth, is simply a representation of great spiritual conditions, of deeper meaning than we can here fathom.

CHAPTER 13.

MAN'S COMMUNION WITH GOD.

Man is not left to himself on the face of the earth. Though his memory has been taken away, he will not be allowed to drift unwatched and unassisted through the journey on earth. At the best, man is only a student who often needs the assistance of a teacher. It is indispensable, therefore, to know how communication may be established by man with intelligent beings wherever they may be.

The Will to Ask. The first of the fundamental principles by which man may confer with God, is that man must show his desire to receive, by asking for help. Man has the right to reject whatever is offered him; in the midst of plenty he may refuse to eat. Therefore, whatever a man gains from the surrounding wisdom is initiated either by a petition or by a receptive attitude which is equivalent to a request. Unless a man ask, he is in no condition to receive, and ordinarily nothing is given him. On extraordinary occasions, when God uses a man to accomplish his purposes, something may be given without the initiatory prayer, but such gifts are rarely of value to the man himself. To get help from without, a man must ask for it. That is the law. History confirms this doctrine. Adam prayed to God and the angel came to explain the plan of salvation. Joseph Smith, the latter-day restorer of the Gospel, prayed in the grove and the Father and the Son appeared. It is unnatural to believe that gifts are given without prayer. That the answer is often overwhelmingly greater than the expressed desire, is only a sign of the love of the Giver, and does not remove the necessity of asking, as the first step in obtaining what a person desires. It is probable that no request, addressed to a being of superior intelligence, is refused. However, the answer comes at a time and place not predetermined by man.

By Personal Appearance. In answer to prayer, God may appear personally. There is no physical or spiritual reason why God should not appear to his children in person whenever he so desires. In fact, sacred history indicates that God appeared to Adam in the Garden of Eden, to Abraham in the Holy Land, to Moses on the mountain, to Joseph in the sacred grove, and to many others at various times during the earth's history. Likewise, Jesus Christ, the Son of God, lived upon this earth and walked and talked with men. To limit the powers of God by saying that he cannot or will not now appear to man, is to make him a creature of less power than is possessed by man.

By the Visitation of Angels. The will of God may be transmitted to man by visible representatives who are beings of a lower degree of intelligence. Angels have frequently visited men and brought to them divine messages concerning their own affairs or the affairs of the world. After Adam was driven out of the Garden of Eden, an angel came and laid before him the philosophy of man's existence. Similarly, angels appeared to Enoch, Noah, Abraham, Moses, Joseph Smith and numerous others, many of which are not recorded in history. These vivid personages, intelligent beings vastly superior to man. knowing well the laws of nature and therefore able to control them, may be with man, though they are not seen with the natural eye. Most probably we walk in the midst of such invisible intelligent spirits. The development from the earth-journey comes largely from the self-efforts of man, who, apparently, must depend upon himself. If at will he could bring to his aid visible, supernatural beings, to tide him over his difficulties, his need of self-development and self-dependence would become very small, and the man would not grow strong.

By the Holy Spirit. God is a personal being of body—a body limited in extent. He cannot, therefore, at a given moment be personally everywhere. Time and space surround him as they surround us. It is difficult to believe that God can in person answer the numberless petitions reaching his throne. Nevertheless, it is known distinctly that God, by his power, will and word is everywhere present. It is almost as difficult to believe that, in spite of the hosts of heavenly beings, personal administrations are possible in the great majority of the countless petitions to God. God must be, therefore, in possession of other agencies whereby his will may be transmitted at his pleasure to the uttermost confines of space. The chief agent employed by God to communicate his will to the universe is the holy spirit, which must not be confused with the Holy Ghost, the personage who is the third member of the Godhead. The holy spirit permeates all the things of the universe, material and spiritual. By the holy spirit the will of God is transmitted. It forms what may be called the great wireless system of communication among the intelligent beings of the universe. The holy spirit vibrates with intelligence; it takes up the word and will of God as given by him or by his personal agents, and transmits the message to the remotest parts of space. By the intelligent domination and infinite extent of the holy spirit, the whole universe is held together and made as one whole. By its means there is no remoteness into which intelligent beings may escape the dominating will of God. By the holy spirit, God is always with us, and "is nearer than breathing, and nearer than hands and feet." The intelligent earthly manifestations of the holy spirit are commonly spoken of as the natural forces. It is conceivable that the thunders and the lightnings, the movements of the heavenly bodies, the ebb and flow of the oceans, and all the phenomena known to man, are only manifestations of the will of God as transmitted and spread by the measureless, inexhaustible, infinite, all-conducting holy spirit.

By the holy spirit, which fills every person, man may obtain information from God. By its means come the messages which transcend the ordinary methods of acquiring knowledge. By it man may readily communicate with God, or God with him. When a person utters his prayer in faith it is impressed upon the holy spirit, and transmitted, so that God may read the man's desire.

This doctrine of a rational theology has been duplicated in a modest way by the development of wireless telegraphy. According to science, the universe is filled with a subtle substance called the ether, on the waves of which the message is spread throughout the universe to be taken up by any person who has the proper receiving apparatus.

The Eternal Record. So thoroughly permeated with the holy spirit is the immensity of space that every act and word and thought is recorded and transmitted everywhere, so that all who know how to read may read. Thus we make an imperishable record of our lives. To those whose lives are ordered well this is a blessed conception; but to those of wicked lives, it is most terrible. He who has the receiving apparatus, in whose hands the key is held, may read from the record of the holy spirit, an imperishable history of all that has occurred during the ages that have passed in the world's history. This solemn thought, that in the bosom of the holy spirit is recorded all that pertains to the universe—our most secret thought and our faintest hope—helps man to walk steadily in the midst of the contending appeals of his life. We can not hide from the Master.

CHAPTER 14.

MAN WALKS WITH GOD.

The knowledge of means of communication between man and God is of great help to man in all the affairs of his life.

Reading God's Message. In possession of the holy spirit is a record of the will of God with respect to all things and all occurrences, great or small, in the universe from the first day. The big problem of man is to read the message of God as it is held by the holy spirit. In wireless telegraphy, a spark coil sets up waves in the ether and other coils similarly "tuned," receive the waves anywhere in the universe. In wireless telegraphy the all-important thing is that the transmitting and receiving instruments be tuned alike, for only then may the message be read. The same principle holds with the holy spirit. The giver and the receiver must be "tuned" alike, that is, must be in harmony, if the messages are to pass readily and understandingly from one to the other. The clearness of the message depends wholly upon the degree to which this tuning approaches perfect harmony.

Spirit Blindness. There are many who, walking among vast spiritual forces, yet feel themselves wholly alone. They do not have the assurance that there is something or someone near them which may not be known by the ordinary judgment of the senses, yet which may be known by man. These

persons are so untuned as to be unable to understand the messages of the holy spirit. Many
will not be brought into an understanding harmony with the holy spirit; others merely find
it so hard to be brought into tune with the
infinite that they would rather be without the
messages than to do the necessary labor of acquiring harmonious relations with the holy spirt.
Those who can not feel and in part commune with
the holy spirit, are blind to the larger part of the
universe, which lies outside of the circumscribed
world, swept by our immediate senses. In terms of
the unseen forces will the earth at last be cleared
of all its mystery. In yesterday and tomorrow shall
today be glorified. The eternal concern of man will
be, as it has been, to secure an understanding
knowledge of all the forces of space. They, therefore, who cannot on this earth possess a direct assurance of the existence and assistance of the great
unseen world, are indeed spiritually blind, and much
to be pitied.

Prayer. As already stated, all communication between man and a higher intelligent Being must be initiated by a request from the man. Thus, the place
of prayer in the life of man is at once established.
Prayer is a request for further light, protection, or
whatever else is desired. Prayer is the first and
greatest means of reading God's messages, for by
intense prayer man gradually places himself in tune
with the infinite so far as his request is concerned.
Those who do not ask, naturally do not establish an
understanding relationship with the unseen world,
and no message appears. The Being of higher intelligence, to whom the request is directed, may or

may not grant the prayer, but some answer will be given. Prayer has been said to be "the soul's sincere desire." Only when it is such will the highest answer be obtained, and it is doubtful if such a prayer is ever refused. No prayer is unheard. The place and time of prayer are of less importance. Morning, noon and night, prayer is always fitting. However, it is well to be orderly, and to beget habits of prayer, and certain hours of the day should therefore be set aside for prayer, both in private and in the family. Frequent and regular prayer helps to remind man of his dependence on a Being of higher intelligence in accomplishing the great work of his heart. A man should pray always; his heart should be full of prayer; he should walk in prayer. Answers will then be heard as God pleases. Seldom is a man greater than his private prayers.

Active Prayer. To become properly tuned with the guiding intelligent Being, one must not pray in a stereotyped way. A man must give himself to the matter devotedly desired, in the form of prayer, and then support it with all his works. Prayer is active and not passive. If a thing is wanted a man must try to secure it. Then, as a man devotes all of himself to the matter of the prayer, his attitude becomes such as to make him susceptible to the answer when it shall be sent. Prayer may be said to be the soul's whole desire.

The Gift of Understanding. Every now and then a man is found who seems to possess a knowledge above that of his fellow men. Knowledge is gained by tremendous self-effort, and the men who know most are usually those who have exerted themselves most to learn. However, it is well known that those who have given themselves with all their might to a certain study, often have great flashes of insight, whereby they leap as it were from knowledge to knowledge, until their progress becomes tremendously rapid, compared with that of ordinary men.

This means of acquiring knowledge may be compared crudely with the switch of an electric lighting system. When the switch is out, though the great dynamo in the canyon mouth hammer and generate its electricity, there is no flow of current through the city system and all is darkness. Yet a man, with a slight effort, can raise the switch and connect the wires, thereby flooding the city with light. The result appears to be infinitely greater than the cause. Thus, those who by great effort build up systems of truth often reach a place where by relatively little effort a flood of new light may be thrown upon the subject to which the mind has given itself. That is one of the compensations to those who strive with all their might for the mastery of any subject. This power becomes the gift of understanding, which may come to all who study deeply.

The gift of understanding is the result of the operation of the holy spirit. The holy spirit which is in communication with the whole universe, is in a measure subject to those who give themselves devotedly and with all their heart to any righteous matter. It is one of the most precious of gifts, and one that should be sought after by all men, because by its aid, the chance for development is greatly increased.

Man Walks with God. Literally, then, through the assistance of the mighty and all-pervading holy spirit, man is, indeed, always in the presence of

God and his agencies. From this point of view
man is immersed in the light and power of Godliness. He, who by earnest prayer, close attention,
and noble desires seeks the intelligence above and
about him is not alone. He walks hand in hand
with intelligent beings and draws from them the
power that he does not of himself possess. In times
of need such a man may reach into the black unknown and bring out hope, born of high knowledge.

Man and the Devil.

CHAPTER 15.

THE KINGDOM OF THE EVIL ONE.

If there is progression, there may also be retro-gression; if there is good, there may be evil. Every-thing has its opposite.

Descending Beings. In a universe contain-ing eternal, intelligent, personalities possessing free agency, there may be beings who are in oppo-sition to the general law of progress. In fact, such opposing intelligent spirits or men have always and everywhere been found. Naturally, those who devote themselves to the opposition of law are waging a hopeless battle, and lose their strength as time goes on. Nevertheless, since many of them have acquired great knowledge before they turn against the truth, they may long continue ac-tive in their opposition to righteousness. The final end of such beings is not known. As they are eternal, it is doubtful if they can ever fully destroy themselves. Nevertheless, as they oppose law, they will at last shrivel up and become as if they were not. Beings who would stand in the way of prog-ress, also use the forces of the universe, as best they can, and must be considered, in the ordering of life, whether in or out of the earth.

The Devil. The number of descending spirits in the universe is not known. In fact, little is known about the whole matter, which probably is for the good of man. The scant knowledge that we have, comes largely from the account of the Great Council.

One of the great spirits there present, proposed to save men without the use of their free agency. When he and his numerous followers failed to secure the adoption of this plan they left the Council, and set themselves thenceforth against the plan adopted by the majority. The leader in this rebellion was Lucifer, said to be a prince of the morning, who, undoubtedly, through much diligence, had acquired a high position among the spirits. Even those of high degree may fall. No man is sure of himself, unless from day to day he can keep the germ of opposition from settling within his breast.

Lucifer and his followers, who fell from the Great Council, are the devil and his angels, possessing definite wills and free agencies, who are still continuing the battle that originated in the heavens. The fundamental conceptions of eternalism, including eternal beings, make reasonable the existence of a personal devil, with personal agents, whose indestructible wills are used to oppose the Great Plan through adherence to which man entered upon his earth career.

Man and the Devil. In a measure, God and all other intelligent beings are affected by the active will of man. If man wills not to be helped by God, it is difficult for God to send him divine help. Even so, in the face of the will of man, the devil has little or no power. It is only when man so wills that he hears fully the voice of God; and it is only when man so wills that he hears the message of the devil. The doctrine that a request must initiate the gift is as true in the relationship that may be established between man and the devil as between man and God. God sends his messages throughout the universe; so does the devil as far as his knowledge permits him.   However, the messages of the evil one need not be heard unless man so desires.   In reality, therefore, man does not need to fear the evil one. He is not a force that can work harm, unless man places himself under the subjection of evil; but, if the devil be allowed a hearing, he may become the master of the man, and lead him downward on the road of retrogression.

The Devil Subject to God.   Though the free agency of man is supreme with respect to himself, under the direction of a perfected intelligence, it must not interfere with the free agencies of others. This law holds for all ascending or descending intelligent beings.   For that reason the devil is subject to God, and is allowed to operate only if he keeps within well-defined limits.   He can suggest ways of iniquity, but he cannot force men to obey his evil designs.   A man who sincerely desires to walk in righteousness need have no fear of the devil.

By the knowledge of opposites, man may draw conclusions of far-reaching importance in his course of progression.   The operations of the devil and his powers may, therefore, serve some good in giving contrasts for man's guidance.   This does not mean that it is necessary for man to accept the suggestions of the evil one, or to commit evil to know truth.   On the contrary, every rational impulse resents the thought that a man must know sin so that he may know righteousness better.   Unfortunately, the works of the evil one may be plentifully observed in the world, among those who have forsaken the Great Plan and the path of progression

Man and the Church.

CHAPTER 16.

WHY A CHURCH?

Those who believe in the Great Plan form the community known as the Church. Many men, who have given the subject only superficial study, find it difficult to understand why a church should be necessary.

Man Helped by God on Earth. It was not intended, in the plan of salvation, that man, though in forgetfulness, should wander alone and helpless through the earth. Rather was it intended and made necessary that men should gain experience by actual contact and contest with the earth and earthly forces, under the watchful care of beings of superior intelligence, who would help as demanded by man's free agency. In an intelligent world it could not well be otherwise. In fact, without the help of superior intelligence, the earth would be chaotic instead of orderly. The Great Plan is founded on intelligence, guided by a God of intelligence, and has for its purpose greater intelligence.

Avenues of communion with God have been pointed out, but many men are impervious to divine messages and need earthly help to understand the will of God. The Church, the community of persons with the same intelligent faith and desire, is the organized agency through which God deals with his children, and through which such help may be given man. Through the Church, God's

mind may be read by all, at least with respect to
the Church community. Moreover, the authority
to act for God must be vested somewhere on earth.
The Church holds this authority for the use of man.
Besides, it is the common law of the universe,
that when intelligent beings are organized, as of one
body, they progress faster, individually and collec-
tively. The Church as an organization represents
God on earth and is the official means of communication between men and God.

The Plan of Salvation for All. In the Great Council the earth-career was planned for all the spirits
there assembled who accepted the Plan. The earth
and whatever pertains to it, are for all and not for
the one or the few. This means that man must
not go through his earth-life independently, doing
as he pleases, living apart from his fellowmen and
accepting the Great Plan in his own way. By his
own free agency he became a member of the hosts
of the earth, and by his own promise, given in the
Great Council, he must live in accordance with definite rules to be enforced by God. The Church is
the community of those who, having accepted the
Plan, desire unitedly to work out their mutual salvation under the settled authority of God.

The purpose of the Great Plan can not be wholly
fulfilled until all have heard the Gospel. The
Church as a body undertakes to carry out this
purpose. Only when the Church is not organized on earth, may individuals who know the Great
Plan, stand alone; but even in such case it is the
bounden duty of those having the knowledge, to
give themselves to the converting of others, so that
the Church may be organized.

Orderliness. If each intelligent being placed on this earth, were to lead an independent life and deal independently with his God, relative to all matters concerning him, many of which would of necessity involve others, there would soon be disorder among humanity. It has been found desirable in all earthly affairs to organize so that order may prevail. By the organization known as a church all things may be done in order. Chaos is abhorrent to the intelligent mind.

Test of Attitude. There is yet another reason for the organization of a church. The plan of salvation is one founded in intelligence. Man must accept and live its laws and ordinances intelligently. The Church, by his adherence to these laws and ordinances, gives a man a means of testing himself as to his attitude towards the whole Plan.· Whatever is done in life somehow connects itself with the Church. A Church which separates itself from the actual, daily life of the man does not acknowledge the essential unity of the universe and is not founded on man's intelligent conceptions of the constitution of the universe. The Church, therefore, must possess a system of laws the compliance with which will enable a man or his fellows to test his progress and spiritual condition, which, in turn, will be a guide for his future work. It would be difficult for a man to apply such tests to himself if he stands alone, away from his fellow men and making laws for himself to fit his apparent needs.

Authority. There is much to be done for man and by man during the earth-career. Every day brings its problems; laws are to be enforced; ordinances to be performed, and God must communicate with his earthly children. Much of this work involves authority, which must be settled somewhere if order is to prevail. The authority to act for God is committed to the Church, as the organized community of believers, and, indeed, authority is a distinguishing characteristic of the Church. Every man has or may receive authority to act in his own behalf in many matters, but to exercise authority in behalf of others, requires the kind of authority which God has delegated to the Church. Some form of authority from God is necessary in all our work, and the earthly source of God's authority is the Church, organized by the supreme, intelligent God.

The Great Purpose of the Church. Finally, the plan of eternal progress involves every living soul who comes upon earth. To the Church is committed the great task of keeping alive this Plan and of carrying it to all the nations. Those who have accepted the truth must be kept active; those who have not accepted it must be taught; all must hear it; even for the dead must the essential ordinances be performed. The Church, then, is a grat missionary organization. This, of itself, justifies the existence of the Church, for it is improbable that any individual would or could undertake the conversion of all the people to eternal truth.

CHAPTER 17.

CONDITIONS OF MEMBERSHIP.

Members of the Church must necessarily accept the conceptions for which it stands. These are, essentially, the plan of salvation, the progressive development of all spirits concerned in the Plan, and the authority of a supreme intelligent Being, to deal with the men and women placed on earth. The conditions of membership are not many, nor difficult to understand. They are, rather, of a kind naturally appearing before an intelligent being concerned in any organization.

Faith. All who enter the Church, or accept the Great Plan must, as a first condition, possess the faith which has been defined as "the substance of things hoped for; the evidence of things not seen." In other words, they must first acknowledge the existence in the universe of things and powers that may not be sensed directly, but which may be used to accomplish the purposes of man. Such an attitude is required to admit the existence of a God or a plan of salvation. Such a faith yields to man a comprehensive possession of the universe, and may establish a philosophy of life that conforms to every law of nature. The man who has no such faith stands before the plan of salvation as before a sealed book. He can not open it, nor opened, can he read it. A faith that admits the universe, seen and unseen, enables man to accomplish great things; in fact, all who have done the great labor of the world, have had such a faith. The law of faith is a general law.

Faith is not necessarily removed from the ordinary experiences of life. On the contrary it is the · beginning of all knowledge. Man observes the phenomena of nature, classifies and groups them until he reaches great general laws representing many individual phenomena. By the use of such laws, reasoning from the known to the unknown, laws may be inferred, the existence of which cannot be sensed directly. By this method of using human knowledge, man rapidly becomes aware of the certainty of the great universe that lies around him but beyond his immediate ken. Moreover, and possibly of chief importance, such inferred but certain knowledge makes man confident that he can continue forever in the acquisition of knowledge and power, and it thus becomes a help in every duty of life.

Repentance. Another fundamental requirement of those who enter the Church is repentance. This is also self-evident, for if man is convinced of the correctness of a certain procedure, that is, if he has faith in it, he certainly will use that faith, if it is to become of any value to him. An active faith is repentance. It is commonly felt that repentance is only the turning away from evil practices. It is probably just as important for man to act out the good he learns as to refrain from doing evil. Repentance, then, is not merely negative; it is also positive. This also is a general law. Great work can be done by those only who have faith and who put that faith into action.

Baptism The third requirement of those who desire entrance into the Church is baptism. The candidate for baptism, presenting himself to one who has authority from Jesus Christ, is buried in the water and taken out again, as a symbol of the death and resurrection, the atoning sacrifice, and the conquest over death, of the Savior. The ordinance of baptism, as far as man is concerned, is essentially an acknowledgment of the atoning sacrifice of Jesus, a promise of obedience to the requirements of the Great Plan, and the acceptance of divine authority. Baptism is also a principle of general application, for in whatever pursuit a man may be engaged, whether in or out of the Church, he must first have faith in the work he has to do, then repent, in the sense of putting his faith into action and, finally, he must give obedience to the laws involved in the work.

The Gift of the Holy Ghost. The fourth condition of Church membership, which is in the nature of a result of the three first requirements, is that the candidate receive the gift of the Holy Ghost. This is accomplished when one having authority places his hands on the head of the candidate, confirms him a member of the Church, and says, "Receive the Holy Ghost." This establishes an authoritative connection between man and God, the Holy Ghost, by which it is possible to secure, through the active support of the Holy Ghost, more light and power and confidence than man may secure unaided. Every man born into the world has life by the holy spirit and may, through its operations, and his own self-effort, be in communication with all other intelligent beings in the universe; but, only

those who conform to the first ordinances of the
Gospel are connected officially with the powers of the
Holy Ghost in such a way as to secure added help.
A distinct and real power comes to the individual
who has received the Holy Ghost. It is as if he had
been given a key to a great and wonderful building
which he enters at his pleasure. However, the key
may be kept unused; then the gift has been of no
value. Man must draw upon the Holy Ghost, if the
gift shall be real. The gift of the Holy Ghost also
represents a general law, for it is evident that all
who have faith made active by repentance, and have
shown obedience by baptism, will be in such harmony with intelligent forces as to receive great
light from them if desired or needed.

Continued Conformity. It is not sufficient that a
man secure entrance into the Church by compliance
with the first four principles of the Gospel. After
he has attained membership he must become active
in the practice of the laws which constitute the body
of Church doctrine, and which are quite as important as the fundamental ones preceding entrance.
Passivity will not suffice; activity only constitutes
an unqualified membership in the Church. The
man will be "in tune" with the work only when he
lives out daily the principles of the Great Plan.
This is self-evident, moreover, because the Church
has the mission of bringing the Gospel to the understanding of all men on earth, and unless the members of the Church are active in missionary work,
they will not acquire the full spirit of the Church.
Unselfishness should characterize the members of
the Church.

Acceptance of Authority. The conditions of membership here mentioned are all vital. Nevertheless, in addition to them, candidates for admission to the Church must acknowledge the full authority of the Church as a divine institution, to which has been committed, by God, the authority to act for him in all matters pertaining to the plan of salvation. Without this authority, the Church is no more than any man-made institution. The acceptance of authority means that all the laws of the Gospel must be obeyed, by every member. The law cannot be varied for individuals, to please their fancies or supposed needs. This is clearly brought out by the historical fact that Adam, after he had been taught and had accepted the Gospel, was baptized, confirmed, and received 'all the ordinances of the Church. Similarly, Jesus, the Son of God, began his official labors by being baptized by one having authority. The pattern has been set for all; and it has been followed in all dispensations. If men be on the full road of progress they will comply with the laws of membership, and become active in the support of the Church and its work.

CHAPTER 18.

THE PRIESTHOOD OF THE CHURCH.

The Priesthood of the Church differs vitally from
that of churches composed only of fragments of the
complete truth.

Priesthood Defined. The Church is composed of
eternal, intelligent beings, moving onward in eternal
progression, who have accepted God's plan of salvation. It is God's Church. God directs the work
of his children on earth, and he naturally gives attention to the Church. Nevertheless, although God
is the directing intelligence, he is not here in person,
nor are other superior beings sent to take charge of
the work, for that would be contrary to the law that
through his free agency and by self-effort, man on
earth must move onward and upward. Therefore,
that the earth-work may be done authoritatively,
God has delegated the necessary authority to man.
The Priesthood is simply the name given this authority. The body of the Priesthood consists of the persons who have received this authority and who may
act for God, on earth, in matters pertaining to the
Church or to themselves. Without authority from
God, there can be no Priesthood.

Divisions of the Priesthood. Much work is to be
done in the Church, and the work differs greatly, for
man's life is complex. Consequently, many and varied
are the labors that must be directed and supported
by the Priesthood. To accomplish the work well,

there must be a division of labor—the fundamental characteristic of all orderly work.

There are two great divisions of the Priesthood, the Aaronic and the Melchizedek, each of which possesses special authority. Each of these divisions is again sub-divided. These divisions and subdivisions are all necessary for the complete exercise of the Priesthood in the Church.

One great division of the Priesthood of God, the Aaronic Priesthood, is named after Aaron, the brother of Moses, a famous leader in this priesthood. It is the Lesser Priesthood, really only an appendage of the Higher or Melchizedek Priesthood. To the Aaronic Priesthood is assigned, particuarly, the temporal work of the Church, but it also has authority to preach, teach and baptize. The Melchizedek Priesthood, named after the great high priest Melchizedek, is the higher division of the Priesthood, and includes the Aaronic Priesthood. It holds the keys of spiritual authority and has the right to officiate under proper direction in all the affairs of the Church. The subdivisions of these Priesthoods make it possible to group, simply and properly, the duties of the members of the Church.

The Aaronic Priesthood. Those who hold the Aaronic Priesthood belong to one of three ascending groups: the deacon, the teacher, and the priest. The bishop presides over the priest's quorum and is the presiding authority of the Aaronic Priesthood. Each group, in addition to its own speical authority, may, when called upon by proper authority, exercise also the authority of the group below it. The members of the Aaronic Priesthood are organized in quorums of twelve deacons, twenty-four teachers and forty-eight priests. Each quorum is presided over by a president and two counselors, which in the priests' quorum are the bishop and his two counselors.

The Melchizedek Priesthood. The Higher Priesthood is characterized by spiritual authority, the right of presidency and the power of officiating in all the work of the Church. There are also several divisions of this Priesthood but the fundamental authority is the same in all, and each division represents merely a calling in the Higher Priesthood. There are five chief groups in this Priesthood; the elder, the seventy, the high priest, the apostle, and the patriarch. The elder may officiate when properly called and set apart in any of these groups of the Priesthood, without having conferred upon him any further Priesthood. The members of the Higher Priesthood are organized into quorums, of 96 elders with a president and two counselors and of 70 seventies with seven presidents. The quorums of high priests are indefinite in number, except administrative quorums, such as the Twelve Apostles and the First Presidency.

All Hold the Priesthood. The Church exists to advance the Great Plan by which, in the end, every man may live happily on earth and at last enter into great progression. In it there should be no active and non-active members, for all must be active to work out their own proper destinies, and to assist in the advancement of the whole Plan. All, therefore, need the authority of the Priesthood to officiate as may be needed in the work of the Church, or in their own behalf. If the work of the Church were delegated to a few members, it would probably be reasonable for a few men to hold the Priesthood. When, however, every member must or should take upon himself a part of the active work of the Church, it is necessary that every man hold the authority of the Priesthood so that he may authoritatively perform the necessary acts in the propaganda of truth.

In fact, in the Church, all men who have attained sufficient experience hold or should hold the Priesthood. The young men are ordained deacons, teachers and priests, and at last elders, when they possess all the authority of the Priesthood. They may then receive an ordination and calling in the Melchizedek Priesthood, such as seventy, apostle, high priest or patriarch.

Women enjoy all the endowments and blessings of the Priesthood in connection with their husbands. The family is the basis of society on earth, and as there must be organization among intelligent beings, someone must be spokesman for the family. In the family, the man is the spokesman and presiding authority, and, therefore, the Priesthood is bestowed upon him.

It is clear that there is no Priesthood class in the Church of Jesus Christ. The Priesthood belongs to all. This is another distinguishing mark of the true Church, which rests its doctrines upon eternal principles as already outlined. The general possession of the Priesthood by all the male members of the Church is only in conformity with the theory of the Gospel, which makes the Plan one of intelligent, united effort under the direction of beings of higher intelligence, and which declares that the highest individual satisfaction can be obtained only when all other individuals are simultaneously advancing.

The Power of the Priesthood. The Priesthood conferred on man carries with it real power to do effective work in behalf of the plan of salvation. Under the normal organization of the Church, when things are moving on in the ordained way, there is no insistent evidence of the great power possessed by those who have the Priesthood, and who, therefore, can act for God in matters pertaining to the Church. Under such a condition there is a quiet, steady use of power in behalf of the daily work of the Church—each man performing the work that has been assigned to him, in addition to which each man in his own behalf may use his authority as seems to him fitting. Yet, the power is with the Priesthood, and when need arises, it becomes the voice of God, which all must hear. As an illustration of the great power, authority and duty carried by the Priesthood it may be recalled that, if by any chance every man holding the Priesthood in the Church should be destroyed, save one elder, it would be the duty and right of that one elder, under divine revelation, to reorganize the whole Church with all the grades of the Priesthood and of its officers. This far-reaching authority is held by all who receive the Priesthood—an authority to be guarded carefully and to be used cautiously as directed.

CHAPTER 19.

THE ORGANIZATION OF THE CHURCH.

To carry on the diversified work of the Church requires a close organization. An organization, in turn, requires officers. All the officers of the Church hold the Priesthood, but the Priesthood is held also by many who do not hold official positions. Therefore, while the authority to act in all the offices of the Church is held by practically every man in the Church, that authority, in the administration of the affairs of the Church, becomes effective only when the man is called to exercise the authority. The chief officers of the Church are herewith briefly enumerated.

The General Authorities. The First Presidency consists of three presiding high priests, a President and two counselors, whose duty it is to supervise the work of the whole Church, in all matters of policy, organization and execution. No part of the work of the Church is beyond their authority. With the death of the President, the First Presidency becomes disorganized.

Associated with the First Presidency is the quorum of Twelve Apostles. The Twelve are special witnesses for Christ, and it is their duty to carry the Gospel to all the world. In addition, they give direct assistance to the First Presidency. When the quorum of the First Presidency is disorganized, the quorum of apostles becomes the presiding quorum until the First Presidency is reorganized. The quorum of the Twelve has one president, who is always the senior apostle.

The Patriarchs of the Church possess the sealing and blessing powers and receive instructions from the Presiding Patriarch.

The quorums of Seventy, the missionary quorums of the Church, are presided over by the Seven Presidents of the first quorum. This Council labors under the direction of the apostles. If the First Presidency and the quorum of the Twelve were disorganized, simultaneously, the first quorum of Seventy would become the presiding quorum until full reorganization were effected.

The temporal affairs of the Church are largely cared for by the Presiding Bishopric, consisting of the presiding bishop and two counselors. The Presiding Bishopric also has general supervision of the bishops of the wards of the Church.

The General Authorities are the First Presidency, the Twelve Apostles, the Presiding Patriarch, the Presidents of the first quorum of Seventy, and the Presiding Bishopric—making in all twenty-six men. These general presiding authorities, representing all the great divisions of the Priesthood, deal with all the general affairs of the Church.

The Stakes of Zion. For convenience of administration, the Church is divided into stakes containing usually from one thousand to ten thousand members. The stakes are presided over by a Stake Presidency, three high priests denominated president and two counselors, which have the same relation to the stake that the First Presidency has to the whole Church. The Stake Presidency are assisted by the high council, consisting of twelve regular and six alternate counselors who are high priests. To this body is assigned much of the work for the welfare of the members of the stake. Such other officers as may be needed are moreover secured in each stake.

The Wards of the Stakes. The stakes are, in turn, divided into wards containing usually from one hundred to two thousand members. They are presided over by a Bishop and two counselors, who are assisted in various capacities by the local ward Priesthood.

The Priesthood in Stakes and Wards. In every ward, if there be enough members, are organized quorums of deacons, teachers, priests, elders and seventies. If there are not enough in one ward to form a quorum, then a quorum is organized from two or more wards. The high priests in a stake are usually assembled into one quorum for the stake. All of the Priesthood meets regularly in the ward to which they belong, for the discussion of their duties and for studying the outlines and books provided by the general Church authorities.

Auxiliary Organizations. In addition to the regular Priesthood, there are helps in government known as auxiliary organizations. These are the Relief Society, for women, the Deseret Sunday School Union, the Young Men's Mutual Improvement Association, the Young Ladies' Mutual Improvement Association, the Primary Association, the Religion Class, the Boards of Education, and others that may be organized from time to time. Each of these is represented by a general board, under the direction of the First Presidency. In each stake there are also stake boards of these auxiliary organizations, under the direction of the stake presidency. Moreover, in each ward of the Church, if large enough, is an organization of each of the auxiliary activities of the Church.

All Must Work. So complete an organization, ramifying throughout the Church, shows that all members of the Church should or may be at work. There is no place for the idler. Every man or woman, who is not averse to working in behalf of the Church, will find some duty that will fill his life.

The Tenure of Office. The officers of the Priesthood have no definite tenure of office. Since all hold the Priesthood, there is always a supply of ready material to fill any vacancies that may occur. The general authorities in the Church have generally held life positions, but a number of these, for various reasons, chiefly insubordination or error of doctrine, have been released before death. According to doctrine, no office in the Priesthood, is absolutely certain of life tenure. Failure to perform properly the work of the office constitutes full cause for removal.

An Unpaid Ministry. The rewards of life should be and are only in part material. To assist, officially, in carrying out the Great Plan, brings its own distinct reward. The Priesthood of the Church, therefore, is largely unpaid. A man's duty in the Priesthood seldom takes all of his time, thus leaving him partly free to earn a livelihood by the use of his profession. When a man's whole time is taken by the Church, he gets his support from the Church. There is no Priesthood class, especially trained for the work, and striving for positions carrying with them high material remuneration. All should know the Gospel and be prepared to carry on the work.

Appointments in the Priesthood. The power to nominate men to fill the official positions in the Priesthood belongs to the Priesthood of the Church. Men are chosen from any walk in life, without previous warning, and the acceptance of the office often means the sacrifice of business, profession, or ease of life. Under this system there can be no talk of men seeking offices in the Church. Preparation to do the work of the Church can be the only form of self-seeking, and that may or may not lead to any particular position in the Church. Meanwhile, the vast organization of the Church is such as to find work for every man; and in fact, every worthy worker should be kept busily engaged in the work of the Great Plan.

Common Consent. Every officer of the Priesthood, though properly nominated, holds his position in the Church only with the consent of the people. Officers may be nominated by the presidency of the Church, but unless the people accept them as their officials, they can not exercise the authority of the offices to which they have been called. All things in the Church must be done by common consent. This makes the people, men and women, under God, the rulers of the Church. Even the President of the Church, before he can fully enter upon his duties, must be sustained by the people. It is the common custom in the Church to vote on the officers in the general, stake and ward conferences. This gives every member an opportunity to vote for or against the officers. Meanwhile, the judiciary system of the Church is such that there is ample provision whereby any officer of the Church, if found in error, may be brought to justice and if found guilty be removed from his position.

The doctrine of common consent is fundamental in the Church; and is coincident with the fact that the Church belongs to all the people. Since the authority of the Priesthood is vested in all the people, it follows that the officials of the Priesthood must be responsible to the people. The responsibility and work of the Church are not only for but by the people as a whole.

Bestowal of the Priesthood. On the earth the Priesthood was first conferred on Adam and was handed down directy from Adam through his descendants to Noah. Every link in this progression of the Priesthood has been preserved. Similarly, after Noah, it was continued for many generations. Moreover, Jesus conferred the Priesthood directly upon his disciples. At various times in the history of the world, the Priesthood has been given by God to man and continued for various lengths of time. In these latter days of the restored Church, John the Baptist appeared in person and conferred the Aaronic Priesthood upon Joseph Smith and Oliver Cowdery. Later, Peter, James and John, who had received the Priesthood from Jesus Christ,.and who represented the Presidency of the Priesthood in those days, appeared to Joseph Smith and Oliver Cowdery and conferred upon them the Holy Priesthood and the apostleship which carried with it authority in the lower divisions of the Priesthood. In the Church of Christ the authority of the Priesthood may always be traced back directly to God, from whom it radiates and whom it represents.

CHAPTER 20.

THE AUTHORITY OF THE PRIESTHOOD.

The authority of the Priesthood is often misunderstood, and it is frequently the rock upon which many men and women suffer spiritual shipwreck.

The Foundation of Authority. The power or right to command or to act, is authority. In the beginning, man, conscious and in possession of will, reached out for truth, and gained new knowledge. Gradually as his intelligence grew, he learned to control natural forces, as he met them on his way. Knowledge, properly used, became power; and intelligent knowledge is the ony true foundation of authority. The more intelligence a man possesses the more authority he may exercise. Hence, "the glory of God is intelligence." This should be clear in the minds of all who exercise authority.

Abolute Authority. Such high authority, based on increasing intelligent knowledge, may be called absolute authority. All other forms of authority, and many forms exist, must be derived from absolute authority, for it is the essence of all authority. Nothing in the universe is absolutely understood, and absolute authority does not mean that full knowledge or full power has been gained over anything in the universe. Forever will the universe reveal its secrets. By absolute authority is meant the kind of authority that results directly from an intelligent understanding of the things over which authority is exercised.

Authority can therefore, be absolute only so far as knowledge goes, and will become more absolute as more knowledge is obtained. · The laws of God are never arbitrary; they are always founded on truth.

Derived Authority. Anyone possessing the absolute authority resting on high intelligence, will often find it necessary or convenient to ask others to exercise that authority for him. This may be called derived authority. It does not necessarily follow that those who are so asked understand the full meaning of the authority that they exercise. The workman in a factory carries out the operations as directed by the chief technician, and obtains the same results, though he does not to the same extent understand the principles involved.

Every person who has risen to the earth-estate possesses a certain degree of absolute authority, for he has knowledge of nature which gives him control over many surrounding forces. Every person possesses or should possess certain derived authority, which is exercised under the direction of a superior intelligence, though it is not always wholly understood.

The Authority of Office. In an organized body like the Church, each activity must be governed by established laws. Those who have been chosen officers to enforce these laws and to carry on the regular work of the Church, exercise their power because of their office. Authority of office is only a form of derived authority—derived from the people who have agreed to submit their wills to certain officers, who are to enforce laws accepted by the people. Even such authority, belonging to official positions, must be founded on intelligent knowledge.

and the organization of the Church itself must be intelligently authoritative. Therefore, authority of office is best exercised when those holding it have qualified themselves intelligently for the work. The mistakes made by officers are commonly due to the want of the needed intelligence in the exercise of their duties. Fortunately, however, the Church is so organized that the actions of its officials may be tried for their righteousness whenever they appear to be wrong to the people. Mistakes are most likely to be made by officials who will not qualify themselves for their work.

Authority and Free Agency. While intelligent knowledge does establish the highest degree of authority, absolute authority, yet it does not, alone, justify the exercising of authority that may conflict with the wills of others. The law of free agency must not be transcended; nor is it permissible to do anything that will hinder, in the least, the progress of man under the Great law. Authority must therefore be exercised only in such a manner as to benefit other individuals. Naturally, when a community accepts a body of laws for their government, and officers are appointed by the people to enforce the laws, the punishment of the disobedient is not an interference with free agency, for all have accepted the law. Only when a person withdraws from the community, does the community law become inoperative with respect to him. Since the battle for free agency must not be waged again, laws must be enforced as they are accepted by the people; thus it comes about that all the officers in the Church, who merely represent the people, must be sustained by the people. The people govern the

Church through their sustained authorities. When a person opposes righteousness, the worst that can be done is to sever that individual from the organization. The Priesthood has no authority to exercise further punishment. The punishment which comes to those who do wrong is automatic, and will, of itself, find out the sinner.

Authority over Self. The Priesthood conferred on man establishes an authority which each man may at all times exercise with respect to himself and God. By the authority of the Priesthood he has a right to commune with God in prayer or in other ways, and has, as it were, the right to receive communications in return from the intelligent beings' about him, so that his ways may be ways of strength and pleasantness. Man's own work should be inseparably connected with the power of the Priesthood to which he has attained.

The Exercise of Authority. The authority committed to man by God is in earthly hands. The flesh is weak; and men who possess authority may often make mistakes in its exercise. The proper manner of exercising the authority of the Priesthood has been made exceedingly clear. "The rights of the Priesthood are inseparably connected with the powers of heaven, and the powers of heaven cannot be controlled or handled only upon the principles of righteousness. That they may be conferred upon us, it is true; but when we undertake to cover our sins, or to gratify our pride, our vain ambition, or to exercise control, or dominion, or compulsion, upon the souls of the children of men, in any degree of unrighteousness, behold, the heavens with-

draw themselves; the Spirit of the Lord is grieved;
and when it is withdrawn, Amen to the Priesthood,
or the authority of that man. Behold! ere he is
aware, he is left unto himself, to kick against the
pricks; to persecute the Saints, and to fight against
God. No power or influence can or ought to be
maintained by virtue of the Priesthood, only by per-
suasion, by long-suffering, by gentleness, and meek-
ness, and by love unfeigned; by kindness, and pure
knowledge, which shall greatly enlarge the soul
without hypocrisy, and without guile, reproving be-
times with sharpness, when moved upon by the
Holy Ghost, and then showing forth afterwards an
increase of love toward him whom thou hast re-
proved, lest he esteem thee to be his enemy; that he
may know that thy faithfulness is stronger than the
cords of death; let thy bowels also be full of charity
towards all men, and to the household of faith, and
let virtue garnish thy thoughts unceasingly, then
shall thy confidence wax strong in the presence of
God, and the doctrine of the Priesthood shall distil
upon thy soul as the dews from heaven. The Holy
Ghost shall be thy constant companion, and thy
sceptre an unchanging sceptre of righteousness and
truth, and thy dominion shall be an everlasting dominion, and without compulsory means it shall flow
unto thee for ever and ever."

Any authority of the Priesthood otherwise exercised than as above stated is not in harmony with
the law. There is therefore no need to fear authority, for those who misuse it will ultimately be removed from their offices and will be punished not
only by the laws of the Church, but by God, the

Giver of law. Meanwhile, the thought stands out .
prominently, that those who are given the Priesthood, and especially those who are to exercise authority in the offices of the Priesthood, should carefully fit themselves for the work that they have to
do. This is the only safe key to authority.

The Unrighteous Exercise of Authority. Authority may be unrighteously exercised from the lack
of intelligence or because of wickedness. Should a
member of the Church note this, the procedure of
correction is to notify the ward teachers, who try
to settle the difficulty. If the ward teachers do not
succeed in this, the bishop's court takes up the
matter, which, if needs be, it passes to the Stake
Presidency and high council, and may be appealed
to the First Presidency. Justice is meted out to all
in the Church. If the people are dissatisfied with
any officer they may refuse to sustain him at the
times of the voting, which prevents him from exercising the functions of his office. However, in all
things the majority rules; and in many of the judg-
ments of the Church there must be unanimity.

The Church Authoritative. The Church of Christ
possesses real authority, derived from God, and in
its work represents God. Such a Church, alone, can
appeal to the human understanding. A Church without authority is limp and helpless. Authority is
the final test of a true Church. Does it attempt to
officiate for God? Does its Priesthood possess authority? From the beginning, the Church of God
has been given direct, divine authority so that its
work might not be questioned. The angel walked
with Adam, God spoke to Abraham, Jesus in person

came on earth, the Father and the Son came to Joseph Smith,—in all ages, when the Church has been fully established, the Priesthood has been conferred by authoritative beings. The authority of the Church is real and genuine and possesses power. By its power it shall be known.

CHAPTER 21.

OBEDIENCE.

In the consideration of Priesthood and its authority, much useless discussion is often indulged in as to whether a person should yield obedience to authority. Some believe that to yield obedience is to lay down free agency.

The Restraint of Nature. Countless forces, surrounding man, are interacting in the universe. By no means can he withdraw himself from them. By experience he has learned that control of natural forces is obtained only when their laws are understood. When a certain thing is done in a certain manner, there is a definite, invariable result. No doubt it has often occurred to an intelligent being that he might wish it otherwise; but that is impossible. The only remedy is to comply with existing conditions, acknowledge the restraint of nature, and gaining further knowledge, put law against law, until the purpose of man has been accomplished. This is the process by which intelligent beings have acquired dominion over nature. Such an acknowledgement of the existence of the law of cause and effect does not weaken man; strength lies in an intelligent subjection to rightful restraint, for it has been the condition of progress from the beginning. The recognition of law and the obedience to law are sure signs that intelligent beings are progressing.

An Active Condition. Obedience is an active condition or it could not be a principle of consequence. It is closely akin to repentance. Obedience simply means that whenever a truth is revealed, it is obeyed, which by our previous definition is a phase of repentance. The man who is active in carrying out what he knows is truth, is an obedient man. His active obedience to authority is based on intelligence; and the more knowledge a man has concerning the nature of the law in question, the more thoroughly obedient is he. Obedience is not a characteristic of ignorance.

The Restraint of Man. Obedience to the invariable laws of nature is, usually, considered to be a self-evident necessity. The question of obedience is commonly raised when man exercises authority. Shall a man obey a man? The first consideration in the answer to this question is whether the system which the man in authority represents is based on truth. If so, then intelligent man will be bound to render obedience to the system, even if it is exercised through imperfect man. The second consideration is whether the man is acting within his authority in the organization. This can always be determined, simply, by laying the matter before the bodies constituted to settle such matters. With the exception of the First Presidency, every officer in the Church has a limited jurisdiction. The third consideration is whether the matter to which authority has been applied is at all under the discipline of the organization. No officer in the Church has authority beyond matters that pertain to the Church. Any authority exercised beyond that field is accepted only at the discretion of the individual members of the Church, and should come only in the form of counsel. If yes is the answer to these three considerations, obedience must be rendered by a progressing man. If no is the answer, obedience should not be yielded, but the matter should be tried before the proper courts.

The restraint of man in the exercise of authority derived from eternal laws, is as compelling as the restraint of nature, because they are parts of the same whole.

The Life of Law. Obedience is nothing more than a compliance with truth. Truth is of no consequence to a man if it is not used. The moment truth is used, obedience begins. Man, and the Church to which he belongs, are active organisms, interested in progress. When truth is given them, promises to use that truth should be required, else all is in vain. Lives conforming to law, alone, are moving onward. For that reason, for every gift to man a promise is required, and usually a statement of the punishment that will follow the non-use or misuse of it. Obedience to truth means progress; refusal to use truth means retrogression.

Disobedience. Disobedience may be active or passive. Passive disobedience is not doing what should be done; active disobedience is doing what should not be done. Both may be equally harmful. The main effect of disobedience is to weaken, and finally wreck the man who disobeys law. Disobedience and sin are synonymous.

The Church Worth Having. The only Church worth having is one having authority, resting on intelligence and truth. Such a Church will command obedience. In such a Church, little misunderstandings are easily rectified. Within the laws of the Church, man has absolute, personal freedom. It is so with nature, outside of the Church. Within the laws of nature, man has full freedom. The greatest freedom known to man comes from obedience to law. The greatest punishment conceivable to man comes from opposition to law. This is true with respect to the Church as a community of the saints, and with respect to individual man in the great universe.

CHAPTER 22.

A MISSIONARY CHURCH.

There must be, in every organization, and especially in a Church dedicated to the great philosophy of man's place in the universe, a great .cementing purpose. In the Church of Christ this is the desire to bring about the highest joy for all mankind.

A Church with a Purpose. According to the fundamental doctrines elaborated in previous chapters, the purpose of the earth-career is to assist in man's development, so that he may acquire more power and therefore more joy. In the nature of things, as already explained, it is impossible for an intelligent being to rise to the highest degree of joy unless other like beings move along with him. The Great Plan will be successful only if all or at least a majority of those who accepted it are saved. The Church, a feature of the Great Plan, must have the same main purpose. All must be saved! In fact, the work of the Church cannot be completed until all have at least heard the truth. There can be no talk of a few saved souls at the throne of God, with the many in hell. The great mission of the Church must be to bring all men into the truth. This is the cementing purpose of the Church.

The Hope of Today. However, men are not saved merely by being taught the truth. They must live it in their daily lives. Life, indeed, is an endless succession of days, each of which must be a little larger in development than the preceding one. Each day must be well spent. The Church must help, every day, in all the affairs of the day, from the food man eats to his highest spiritual thought. Each day must be a step onward to the eternal exaltation which he desires. This is the hope of today. To help in this daily work is one of the main parts of the missionary labors of the Church. All the days of all the members must be made happy ones.

Temporal Salvation. In a church based on the principles already outlined there can be no separation between the spiritual and the temporal. There is one universe, of many aspects, to which we belong. There is one Great Plan for us. In the heavens, spiritual things are probably of greatest importance, but on earth, temporal things are of importance. The impossibility of separating things temporal from things spiritual justifies the attempt of the Church to assist in the temporal affairs of its members. In fact, a large part of the missionary labors of the Church must be to better the temporal conditions of its members. Only when the temporal as well as the spiritual life is looked after, can the Church rise to its full opportunity. Only in sound bodies can the spirit experience the highest joy. Only under sound temporal conditions can the Church move on in full gladness.

The Foreign Mission System. In conformity with the cementing missionary spirit of a church, every member of which holds or may hold the Priesthood, it follows that every member of the Church, whether man or woman, may be called to go on a spiritual or temporal mission for the upbuilding of his fellow-men. In harmony with the law of free agency, it is voluntary with the individual, whether he accept or refuse the call. The custom in the Church of today has been that a man go on at least one mission. which varies in length, two or more years. The missionaries not only assist the members already gathered into the Church, but they travel all over the world, preach to all the everlasting Gospel, and bring those who accept the truth into the Church. The main purpose of the Church missionary system is to preach the Gospel to all the members of the human race, so that, as far as possible, none may be left with the excuse that he has not heard the Gospel.

The Home Mission Service. The whole Church, at home, is devoted to the home mission service. The organizations of the Priesthood and the auxiliary organizations, form a network of active service into which every member of the Church may be brought. The home missionary service concerns itself with the spiritual and the temporal side of man's nature and life. The amusements of the young people; the home life of the older people, and the daily duties of all, are made part and parcel of the organized missionary system of the Church.

For the Common Good. The genius of the Church of Christ stands for the common good; hence the ceaseless missionary activity which is the great cementing principle of the Church. Not for the one, not even for the many, but for all, does the Church stand.

CHAPTER 23.

TEMPLE ORDINANCES.

The Church of God has always been characterized by the possession of temples in which the
holiest work of the Gospel has been done. The activities of the Church have, so to speak, centered
about the temples.

Educational. The doctrines of the origin, present
condition and destiny of man should always be well
in the mind of all, for without this knowledge, it is
difficult to comply fully and intelligently with the
laws and ordinances of the Gospel. It has been provided, therefore, that the story of man, from the beginning, at the present, and to the last great day,
shall be given as frequently as may be desired to the
members of the Church. In the temples this information is given, in an organized and correct form,
so that it may not depart from among men and
women. That is, the temples are conservators of
the great truths of the Gospel. To the temples, man
goes to be refreshed in his memory as to the doctrines relative to man and his place in nature. The
endowments given to members of the Church in the
temples are, essentially, courses of instruction relative to man's existence before he came on this
earth, the history of the creation of the earth, the
story of our first earthly parents, the history of the
various dispensations of the Gospel, the meaning of
the sacrifice of Jesus Christ, the story of the restoration of the Gospel, and the means and methods
whereby joy on this earth and exaltation in heaven

may be obtained. To make this large story clear and impressive to all who partake of it, every educational device, so far known to man, is employed; and it is possible that nowhere, outside of the temple, is a more correct pedagogy employed. Every sense of man is appealed to, in order to make the meaning of the Gospel clear, from beginning to end.

Symbolism. Naturally, the very essence of these fundamental truths is not known to man, nor indeed can be. We know things only so far as our senses permit. Whatever is known, is known through symbols. The letters on the written page are but symbols of mighty thoughts that are easily transferred from mind to mind by these symbols. Man lives under a great system of symbolism. Clearly, the mighty, eternal truths encompassing all that man is or may be, cannot be expressed literally, nor is there in the temple any attempt to do this. On the contrary, the great and wonderful temple service is one of mighty symbolism. By the use of symbols of speech, of action, of color, of form, the great truths connected with the story of man are made evident to the mind.

Covenants. The temple service also gives those who take their endowments, special information relative to their conduct upon earth. For instance, men and women are taught to keep themselves free from sin. They must be chaste, virtuous, truthful, unselfish, and so on. Moreover, they are taught that they must devote themselves and all that they have or may have to the great cause of truth, to teaching the everlasting Gospel to their fellowmen, so that the Great Plan may be worked out according to the mind and will of God. In return for this, those who take their endowments make covenants with each other and their God, that they will observe the instructions given, and will carry them out in their daily lives. Thus the work becomes active and vital. It is also explained that the failure to carry out these promises, when once knowledge has been given, will be punished. This is in accordance with the law that provides a penalty for disobedience, as already explained. Only by the use of knowledge will more knowledge be obtained. The whole system of temple worship is very logical.

Blessings. In the course of instruction in the temple, it is emphasized that blessings will follow those who accept the truth, practice it and live Godlike lives. The essence of the endowment service is a blessing. Punishment is not made so prominent, as is the possibility of inviting great blessings by proper obedience to the truths that may be obtained from time to time.

Temple Authority. Perhaps the most glorious ordinances of the temple are those that seal husband and wife and children to each other for time and all eternity. According to the Gospel, the marriage relation does not necessarily cease with death. On the contrary, since sex is eternal, the sex relation may continue to the end of time. Such a union or sealing may be performed only by special authority, which is possessed only by the President of the Church. The President may, however, delegate the authority for longer or shorter times, so that certain temple workers may perform such marriages in the temples of God. Similarly, children who have been born to parents who were not married for time and eternity. may be sealed later to their parents, so that the relationship may be sustained throughout all the ages of eternity.

Moreover, every ordinance belonging to the Church may be performed in the temple. In the temple is a baptismal font, so that the introductory ordinance may be performed; likewise, every other ordinance for the benefit of the Saints may be performed in the holy temple. The work for the dead, as will be explained in chapter 28, is done in the temples, by the living. The vicarious work for the dead, who did not accept the Gospel on earth, forms the bulk of the temple work, since, after the first time, when endowments are taken for himself, a person must do work for the dead when he goes through the temple.

Possible Repetition. The vastness of meaning in the temple worship makes it difficult at once for man to remember and understand it, and only once are the endowments taken for himself by any one person. To refresh his memory, and to place him in close touch with the spirit of the work, a man may enter the temple as frequently as he desires and take endowments for the dead, and in that way both he and the dead are benefited. The temples, then, are means whereby every member of the Church may receive precious endowments, and may be kept in refreshed memory of the Great Plan, which he, with the rest of the human family, is working out. Temple work is the safety of the living and the hope of the dead. At present, temples are in operation in Salt Lake City, St. George, Logan and Manti, all in Utah, and a temple is nearing completion in Cardston, Alberta, Canada.

Man and Man.

CHAPTER 24.

THE BROTHERHOOD OF MAN.

There are many men and women upon the earth. No one faces, alone, the great forces of nature. About him move other men, with whom he must associate. In the Great Plan it is so ordained that men shall dwell together, and this leads to many of the finest applications of the Gospel to the daily life of man.

Common Origin. By the power of God, the spirits of men were born into the spiritual world; thus all became the children of God. In turn, all have been born from the same spiritual estate into the earth estate, from the one earthly ancestor, Adam. All men are therefore of identical origin. Absolute uniformity prevails among the children of men, so far as their origin is concerned.

Common Purposes. The spirits are placed on earth for a common purpose. From the beginning, man has risen to his high estate through the acquisition of power over the natural forces surrounding him. "Man is that he may have joy," is the fundamental purpose of man's activity, whether on or out of the earth. In the Great Council all the spirits which have reached or will reach the earth, were present; and all declared themselves in favor of the Plan. In conformity with this agreement, man is on earth. All desire a closer acquaintance with gross matter, as a means of future power and consequent joy; and all desire that the earth-experience may be accompanied with as much joy as is possible. Consequently, all who are or have been, or will be assembled on earth, have a common purpose. Absolute uniformity prevails among men so far as their fundamental purpose is concerned.

Common Destiny. Likewise, the destiny of all the spirits sent to earth, is the same. Man has ever moved towards eternal life. All new information, every addition of knowledge, has moved him onward, toward perfection and a vision of greater happiness. True, since all men have free agencies, individual wills express themselves in different ways, and no two spirits are therefore at precisely the same point on the upward road. Some are far ahead, some lag behind, each and all according to individual effort. However, throughout the vast eternities, all who are conscientiously moving upward, though it be ever so slowly, will in time reach a point which is absolute perfection to our mortal conceptions. Then, all will seem as if precisely alike. Whether or not we reach a given point at the same time, all men have a common destiny. As far as the destiny of man is concerned, all are alike.

Inter-dependence. Of even greater importance in daily work is the fact that every intelligent being affects every other intelligent being. Every person affects every other person. Through the operation of the Holy Spirit all things are held together. Good or evil may be transmitted from personality to personality; it is impossible to hide from God, and it is equally impossible for us to hide ourselves completely from our fellowmen. No individual action may restrain or retard another individual; but all our actions, thoughts and words must be so guarded that all are advanced. This is as true for the earth-life as it may be for the spiritual life.

Men affect each other; every man is, in a measure, his brother's keeper. There can be no thought of a man going on in life irrespective of the needs or conditions of his fellowmen. The main concern of man must be to find such orderly acts of life as will enable other men to live out their individual wills without interference. All must be benefited, all must be helped. This is the basis of the great system of co-operation. Meanwhile, the inter-dependence of the spirits dwelling on earth, brings men more closely together, and strengthens the friendships from the former spirit estate.

Brothers. The human race is a race of brothers, of the same origin, with the same purposes and with the same destiny, so elaborately inter-dependent that none may move without affecting the others. Any rational theology must recognize this condition, and, as far as it may be able, must make provision for the proper recognition of the brotherhood of man.

CHAPTER 25.

THE EQUALITY OF MAN.

Though the brotherhood of man is supreme, it does not follow that all men are equal in all particulars. This needs careful examination.

The Pre-existent Effort. Men of common origin, and of common destiny, labor on earth under a mutually accepted Plan. Yet, it is not conceivable, that all the spirits who reach the earth have attained the same degree of progress. The pre-existent progress depended upon self-effort; those who exerted their wills most, made the greatest progress; moreover, those who had led the most righteous lives, and had been most careful of their gifts, had acquired greatest strength—consequently, at the time of the Great Council, though the spirits were, in general, of one class, they differed greatly in the details of their attainments, in the righteousness of their lives, in the stability of their purpose, and in their consistent devotion to the great truth of their lives. In one particular they were all alike: by their faithful efforts, they had earned the right to take another step onward and to share in the earth experience.

Most probably, the power acquired in the life before this is transmitted to some degree to the earth-life. We may well believe, therefore, that the differences in the quality and characteristics of men, may be traced, in part at least, to the pre-existent lives.

It is not unthinkable that, in a plan governed by a supreme intelligent Being, since there are differences of advancement, the spirits who come on earth are placed frequently in positions for which they are best fitted. An intelligent ruler would probably use ability where it is most needed. To some extent, therefore, men may have been chosen for this or that work on earth, and, under the law of progression, this small measure of predestination may be accepted. Yet, it must be remembered that predestination can not be compelling. Man's free agency, the great indestructible gift, always remains untrammeled. Therefore, whatever may be God's plan for man, however easy may be the path to the predestined earth position, the man may at any time, by the exercise of his free agency, depart from the appointed path and enter other fields. Any opposite doctrine is the one proposed by Lucifer in the Great Council.

It is most likely that those who, on earth, accept the highest truth of life, find the Gospel attractive, and are most faithful in the recognition of law, are those who, in the pre-existent state, were most intelligent and obedient. In that sense, the Church consists of God's chosen people—chosen because of their willingness to obey.

The Earth Effort. Nevertheless, the thought that power is drawn from our pre-existent state need not be an overwhelming feeling to oppress and crush us. Our previous life can not be an insurmountable hindrance. The invariable law of cause and effect will enable those who exert themselves on earth to draw great power unto themselves, even so that it may be possible by earth efforts to overcome possible handicaps from pre-existent lethargy. Thus, on earth, man may gain more than he has lost before. Our earth efforts are of greatest consequence. Neither forward nor backward must we look, except to place ourselves properly in our day, but must use in full degree the possibilities of each day as it comes. Man's inequality comes chiefly from the inequality of earth effort.

The Variety of Gifts. Meanwhile, it is always to be remembered that the spirit within must speak through a mortal body, subject to disease and death. The eternal spirit cannot rise here above the conditions of the body, which is of the earth, and is a result of all the physical good and evil to which man has given himself since the days of Adam. During the long history of the race, both strength and weakness have no doubt been added to the body. It possesses inborn, inherent qualities, which man finds it difficult to ignore. Under the best conditions, the body is weaker than the spirit within. It is likely that the spirit within the finest earthly body is infinitely greater than may be expressed through the body. We live only as our bodies allow; and, since our bodies differ greatly, there is in them another source of man's inequality. In fact, the inequality of man comes largely from inequality of body, through which the eternal spirit tries in vain to speak.

The Equality of Opportunity. Clearly, an absolute equality among men is not conceivable, for the differences among the powers of men are infinite in number. We are brothers, but we are occupying a variety of stages of progress. Probably, it is well

that there are such differences, so that by contrast
with each other we may be impelled onward. The
equality of man on earth must be the equal opportunity to progress. From the point in the eternal
journey that each man now occupies, he must be allowed to move onward, unhindered by other persons, and must be allowed to exert his inborn
powers to the full, for his help on the journey. None
must stand in another's way. On the contrary, the
spirit of the Gospel makes clear that the Great Plan
cannot be fulfilled, the earth's destiny cannot be
completed, and our highest progressive rewards
cannot be obtained until all the spirits of man have
been brought under the Gospel rule. Whether on
this earth, or in the future, the work will not be
completed until all have accepted the freedom of the
Gospel. Instead of hindering each other, men must
give each other all possible needed help, then we
offer our fellows an equal opportunity to advance,
and all are helped. With equality of opportunity,
all may advance so far that, in time, the differences
between men will not be apparent.

The equality of opportunity which characterizes
the plan of salvation is shown in the fact that all
the ordinances of the Church, from the highest to
the lowest, are available to every person who enters
the Church. Faith, repentance, baptism and the
gift of the Holy Ghost are, for all, the four cardinal
principles for active participation in the work of
the Church, irrespective of the powers of men. The
endowments of the temple, and all the blessings that
may there be received, are available to every member of the Church who has shown himslf active in

the faith.   In fundamental principles, in gifts and blessings, in spiritual opportunities, as required or offered by the Church, men are stripped of all differences, and stand as if they were equal before God. This is equality of opportunity.

Unequal Equality. Though equality of opportunity be granted all, the wills of men, as expressed through their free agencies, differ greatly.   Consequently, some will use well their opportunities; others will use them poorly.   Under this condition, even if all started out absolutely alike, differences would soon appear.   Without violating the fundamental laws of nature, this seems to be absolutely unpreventable.   Men may soon be grouped as representing different degrees of strength.

However, that the equality of opportunity, belonging to the Great Plan, may be preserved, it becomes necessary for all, whether weak or strong, to support each other.   Differing attainments must be forgotten in the desire to permit all to develop their powers to the utmost, and thus to achieve joy both here and hereafter.   The great problem of every age is how to keep together, as one body, the many who, because of their differing wills, have become different in their powers and attainments.

The Test of Equality.   A test may be applied whereby men may be placed in one class, irrespective of their various attainments.   If a man use his powers, with all his might, for his own and others' good, in the cause of universal progress, he is the equal of every other man of like effort.   No more can be asked of a man.   It is well that humanity, dwelling together, should keep this principle in mind. Men must not be judged, wholly, by their attainments, or by their gifts, but largely by the degree to which they give themselves to the great cause represented by the plan of the major intelligent Being, for the minor intelligent beings of the universe.

CHAPTER 26.

MUTUAL SUPPORT.

The doctrines set forth indicate that each man must exert himself to the utmost. Even this is not sufficient for the full progress of individuals. Every man must also be supported by every other man. Unless this is done, the individual and the community will be retarded.

The Duty of the Strong. The man who is in possession of strength, acquired by any means whatsoever, is under special obligations to the community. The strong must, somehow, attach to themselves those who are weak; and as the strong move onward, they must pull with them those who are weak. If a person possess knowledge, he must give knowledge to others, so that all may attain great knowledge; if he have great faith, he must use faith until all may know its virtue; if he have acquired great wealth, he must use it so that many may share in its physical benefits. Those who have must give to those who have not. Those who understand the deeper, inner life must not forget those who are not gifted with an understanding of the contents of the vast universe.

The weak have similar responsibilities devolving upon them. Under earthly conditions the weak tend to foster jealousy of the strong. This is out of harmony with the law of progress. The weak must seek strength for themselves, and should invite the assistance of the strong. The weak may help the progress of the race by accepting, as a gift, the assistance of the strong. There is no shame in accepting gifts, in learning from those who have more than we have, providing our own powers are used to the full. If the strong will not give to the weak, in the right spirit of helpfulness; or if the weak will not accept the help proffered for their advancement, the whole onward movement will be slowed down.

Moreover, it is a common law of nature that those who are strong, and give of their strength to others, add thereby to their own strength.

Co-operation. Co-operation of all, weak or strong, is characteristic of mutual helpfulness. When many men unite to accomplish great works, mighty results follow. Each man then obtains his full reward. Even if the co-operation provides that its results are divided equally among the participants, the strong receives his full reward, for, because of his greater strength, he has done greater labor, and has consequently added greatly to his strength. The weak, by their association with the strong, having shared equally with them, have gained greater hope, and more courage to carry on their individual work of progress. The principle of co-operation is in full conformity with the whole plan of salvation.

Education. Education looms large in the matter of mutual support, for it is only by the development of individual power that man may help his fellow man and thus recognize the full brotherhood of man. Great powers can be exercised only by faculties that are trained to the utmost. Schools are provided, where the young mind may be guided rapidly and well into a better control of itself. A rational theology must be established upon the basis of developed intelligence, which justifies the existence of schools and other devices for the proper unfolding of the mind. In the Church there must ever be a vigorous propaganda for the education of the masses. The Church must be a generally educated Church, in which the "educated class" includes all.

CHAPTER 27.

THE UNITED ORDER.

The true relation among men, the doctrine of the brotherhood of man, is nowhere better exemplified than in the principle of the united order. This system of living represents, no doubt, the acme of brotherly love and human efficiency.

Purpose. The united order recognizes that men have different talents and therefore different aspirations which should be allowed full and free unfolding. That is, the individual should be allowed to exercise his inborn gifts. The united order further provides that the members of a community share equally in the material returns of the activities of the whole community. Since the wants of a community are satisfied only by a variety of necessary labor, some yielding large, others small, material gains, the united order provides that, if a man work to the full of his ability, all the working days of his life, he should have an equal share in the material gains of the community, whatever his labor may be. Under this system there could be no poverty; all would be amply supplied with the material necessities of life. Those who, because of their greater talents or training, do the greater work, will receive whatever is needed for the maintenance of life; and they will attain, moreover, a greater growth and satisfaction because of the greater work that they have performed. Since the material wants of all will be amply supplied, there can be no real reason why all should not share in the total results of the labor of the community. The united order implies a closely organized body of men and women working together for individual and for mutual advancement. In theory, at least, it appears to be the best answer to many of the great questions that trouble mankind.

Historical. The united order is not a new conception. It has been known from the beginning of time. In the days of Enoch, the seventh patriarch, the united order was practiced successfully. When the Church was organized by Christ, the united order was practiced very fully for some time, by many of the people. It is quite possible that the order has been established and practiced successfully at other times, but no record has come down to this age. Finally, in this dispensation, the united order was revealed to the Prophet Joseph Smith. The people, on several occasions, tried to practice it, and wherever practiced correctly, it appeared to result in good; but individual selfishness usually resulted in the abandonment of the practice. It is a system of life requiring the fullest understanding of the Gospel truth, and the greatest conception of man's place in the universe. In its practice, men must overcome their selfishness, and accept at their true values, the various rewards of life. Enoch and his people acquired such high control over themselves that they were able to practice the united order unselfishly, and at last were translated from the earth without tasting death. It seems that the united order is above the reach of the kind of men and women we now are. Nevertheless, it is the system we approach, as we approach perfection.

Co-operation. The united order has been suspended as a required form of life in the Church, but its spirit still remains. Those who are indeed wortny members of the Church must accept the spirit of the united order. It finds present expression in the system of co-operation, under which many unite in one enterprise, in such a way that no one person dominates it, but that all concerned have a voice in it, and so that the profits resulting from the enterprise are divided more or less uniformly among those connected with it. Co-operative enterprises have been fostered constantly and consistently by the Church in the latter days, and in the majority of instances have been extremely successful. In fact, when the Church settled in Utah, it would have been impossible to accomplish the great work before the pioneers, had they not practiced co-operation. To give every man a full and proper chance is the spirit of the true Church.

Tithing. Every organized Church must have some means of material support. Houses of worship must be constructed; temples must be built; education must be fostered; the poor must be provided for; and many other material needs form a part of the great spiritual mission of the Church. For the general support, therefore, of the Church and of the poor who are unable to provide for themselves, a fund has been provided by the tithing of the people. This is a preparation for the united order, and some day will be replaced by the more complete system. This fund is maintained by the payment, by each member of the Church, of one-tenth of his earnings, as they are delivered to him. The money thus obtained is placed in the hands of the bishops, and is disbursed under the direction of the First Presidency associated with the presiding bishopric and other officials named in the revelations.

Tithing is an ancient system, frequently mentioned in the history of the past. It is fair to all the people, for it is necessarily a system whereby each man pays in proportion to his earnings. Great blessings follow obedience either to the law of united order or the law of tithing.

Voluntary Offerings. In addition to tithing, voluntary offerings may be made to the Church for specific or general purposes, as for the support of the poor or distressed living near us, or for the building of churches.

The Common Good. All these devices for gathering material funds for the sustenance of the Church, simply show the underlying and overwhelming desire of those who understand the Gospel, to assist for mutual benefit. Not the good of one, but the common good, is uppermost in the minds of those who understand and love the Gospel.

CHAPTER 28.

WORK FOR THE DEAD.

The doctrine of the brotherhood of man and the principles of united order and co-operation show the necessity of giving ourselves for the common good. This intense desire of the Church for service to all, for human brotherhood, are probably nowhere better shown than in the work for the dead.

All Must Be Saved. Temple work rests on the principle of the Great Plan that all must be saved, or at least given the opportunity of salvation. Persons who have been unable to accept the Gospel ordinances on earth, are not necessarily denied the privileges of membership in the Church or refused the blessings which come to those who accept the truth. For such dead persons vicarious work must be done in all the essential ordinances of the Church. Vicarious work is not new, for it has been practiced in various forms from the first day. In common daily life, a man is given authority to do official work for another, when a "power of attorney" is conferred. The work of Jesus Christ was essentially vicarious, for he atoned for the act of Adam.

Earthly Ordinances. Great, eternal truths make up the Gospel plan. All regulations for man's earthly guidance have their eternal spiritual counterparts. The earthly ordinances of the Gospel are themselves the reflections of heavenly ordinances. For instance, baptism, the gift of the Holy Ghost and temple work are really earthly symbols of realities that prevail throughout the universe; but, they are symbols of truths that must be recognized if the Great Plan is to be fulfilled. The acceptance of these earthly symbols is part and parcel of correct earth-life, and being earthly symbols they are distinctly of the earth, and can not be performed elsewhere than on earth. In order that absolute fairness may prevail and eternal justice may be satisfied, all men to attain the fulness of their joy must accept these earthly ordinances. There is no water baptism in the next estate, nor any conferring of the gift of the Holy Ghost by the laying on of earthly hands. The equivalents of these ordinances prevail no doubt in every estate, but only as they are given on this earth can they be made to aid, in their onward progress, those who have dwelt on earth. For that reason those who have departed this life without having accepted the earthly ordinances, which constitute in part the conditions of entrance to the Church, must have that work done for them on earth. By proxy they must be baptized by water, receive the laying on of hands and accept of the temple ordinances. By this method the path to eternal life is invariable; in fairness and without discrimination, all must tread it. Were there any departure from this order, it would be a short time only until men might take upon themselves the authority of devising various methods whereby eternal joy might be obtained. This would be unnatural, because definite order prevails throughout nature.

A Work of Love. To do work for the dead involves much sacrifice on the part of the living. Genealogies must be collected, exact information concerning dates of births and deaths and other fundamental data must be obtained, and the better part of a day is required to take the endowments for each dead person—and all this, usually, for a person long dead, of whom the worker may have no definite knowledge beyond name and time of his life. It follows that only by love for one's fellowmen can the work be done. Young and old may do work for the dead in the temples; and young and old are, indeed, engaged in it. Especially in the evening of life, when time is more plentiful for such work, do many persons give themselves fully to this labor of love. As a result of temple work for the dead, to which thousands of people give their time and means, a great flood of love for humanity is poured out upon the people.

The Need of Records. Before the earth passes away into its next stage of existence, work must be done in the temples for all the living and all the dead. Only when this is done, will the curtain be rolled up, and the vision of complete existence given to man. To do work for the dead, who in life did not accept the Gospel, will require complete genealogies of the human race. To secure these is a gigantic task. The diverse conditions of human life, and the vicissitudes of the race have been such that frequently genealogies have not been written and often have been lost. The most careful search of man will not reveal them all. However, as has been explained, in an intelligent universe, nothing is wholly lost. The record of every man exists and by some means will be found before the work on earth is completed. Meanwhile, no external power will come to man's aid, until he has used his own efforts, and therefore it becomes necessary for men to search out existing genealogies of the human race. When that has been done, in the years to come, man may rest secure that the gods who direct our earth, will come to the rescue of this important part of the work of salvation.

Consequently there is intense interest in the Church in all genealogical matters. Every person is on the lookout for his own genealogy; when that is completed, he searches for those of others. Such work intensifies family loyalty and devotion, from which virtues proceed. It follows, also, that the Church records and preserves with utmost care the genealogical histories of its members. Sacred history shows that at all times, when the Church has been on earth, genealogies have been carefully kept and recorded.

The Result. Work for the dead has far-reaching results. First of all. it establishes a close communion among those who have lived and who are living on earth. The hearts of the children are turned to the fathers, and the hearts of the fathers are turned to the children. This, indeed, is the vital principle of the Great Plan—that all may work together to the ultimate good of each.

The principle of infinite, loving brotherhood among men, as exemplified in the work for the dead, may be applied in the daily lives of the living. If so much work is done, so much time and energy expended and so much care bestowed upon the salvation of the dead, how much more should we help and support and love the living. The living must always be man's first concern. This principle, carried into our daily lives. means that we must continually and at our own sacrifice help each other. Then only will the sacrifice for the dead not be in vain.

Work for the dead is no doubt symbolic of the great universal law that things of the universe move onward together, not singly. So great is this principle in its application to daily life, among the living, that it rises to be one of the mightiest principles that contribute to human brotherhood and brotherly **love.**

CHAPTER 29.

MARRIAGE.

We are not the last spirits to enter upon the earth career. There are yet countless numbers of unborn spirits waiting for the privilege of receiving earthly bodies and of tasting the sorrows and the joys of earth. The living, who understand the Great Plan, must not then confine their attention to themselves and to those who have gone before. The waiting spirits must be a concern of our lives.

Eternity of Sex. It has already been said that sex is an eternal principle. The equivalent of sex has always existed and will continue forever. As the sex relation, then, represents an eternal condition, the begetting of children is coincidently an eternal necessity. We were begotten into the spirit world by God the Father, and have been born into the world which we now possess.

The Waiting Spirits. According to the Great Plan, all who, in the Great Council, accepted the Christ, will in time appear on earth, clothed with mortal bodies. All these spirits must be born as children into the world. A high purpose, if not the main one, of the earth work must be, therefore, to continue the race by begetting children and properly caring for them until they reach maturity. Undoubtedly, the waiting spirits are hoping patiently for their turn to reach the earth—a glorious step in the progressive advancement of man, which the spirits have earned by their righteous lives.

The Meaning of the First Command. This doctrine makes clear the meaning of the first great command, to multiply and replenish the earth. It is not only for the joy and satisfaction of humanity that the sex relation, with the possibility of begetting offspring, prevails on earth, but as much for the fulfilment of the eternal Great Plan. It becomes a necessary duty, for all wedded persons who dwell on earth, to bring children into the world. This is the greatest and holiest and most necessary mission of man, with respect to the waiting spirits. Fatherhood and motherhood become glorified in the light of the eternal plan of salvation.

The doctrine that wedded man and woman should not beget children or should limit the number of children born to them, is contrary to the spirit of the Great Plan, and is a most erroneous one. Let the waiting spirits come! Let children be born into the earth! Let fatherhood and motherhood be the most honored of all the professions on earth! Marriage resulting in parenthood is a great evidence of the reality of the brotherhood of man, of the unselfishness of man. However, only in the marriage relation should children be begotten. Looseness of life, between man and woman, is the most terrible of human iniquities, for it leads, assuredly, to the physical decay of the race. With the sanction of the Priesthood, men and women should contract to live together as husband and wife.

The Family. The unit of society is the family. The family circle is intimate, and in it the keenest human loves prevail. As the family develops so will society, as a whole, develop. By children comes complete family life. Without children, family life

is incomplete.   Children are, then, a real necessity in the fulfilling of the possibilities of the
Church.   The true Church always encourages the
begetting of children; the intensifying of family life,
and the dignifying of all the duties pertaining to
procreation.

Celestial Marriage. If sex is eternal, it follows
of necessity, that the marriage covenant may
also be eternal.   It is not a far step to the doctrine
that after the earth work has been completed, and
exaltation in the next estate has been attained, one
of the chief duties of men and women will be to beget spiritual children.   These spirits, in turn, in the
process of time, will come down upon an earth,
there to obtain an acquaintance with gross matter, and through the possession of earthly bodies
to control more fully, and forever, the manifold forces surrounding them.   It is one of the rewards of intelligent development, that we may be
to other spiritual beings, what our God has been
to us.

Among those who understand the Gospel, marriage may be, and indeed should be, for time and
eternity.   Marriage that lasts only during the earth
life is a sad one, for the love established between
man and woman, as they live together and rear their
family, does not wish to die, but to live to grow
richer with the eternal years.   Marriage for time
and eternity establishes a unique relation between
husband and wife.   Their children belong to them
for time and eternity; the family is continued from
this earth into the next life, and becomes a unit in
the eternal life, and, in all family relations, the vision

is cast forward, in anticipation of an undying relationship.

The Sealing Powers. Naturally, the power to seal men and women to each other, for time and eternity, and to seal children to their parents for eternal ages, is a supreme power, committed to man's keeping. The President of the Church is the only person on the earth who holds the keys of these sealing ordinances. True, he may delegate his power to workers in the temples, so that celestial marriages and sealings may go on, but such delegated authority may be withdrawn at any moment. In that respect, it differs wholly from the power of the Priesthood, which can be withdrawn from a man only who is found in sin. It is proper that only one man should hold this power, for it is of infinite effect, and should be guarded with the most jealous care, and kept from the frail prejudices and jealousies of men.

The power to bind for time and eternity is the power, also, to loose that which has been bound, should it be found necessary. Undoubtedly, under human conditions, mistakes may be made, but if such mistakes are made and are not rectified on earth, they will, no doubt, under a supervising intelligent Being, be rectified in the hereafter. It is, however, only through the sealing power that the eternal relationship of the sexes, the eternal increase of life, and the consequent eternal joy, may be obtained.

CHAPTER 30.

THE COMMUNITY.

The relations of the few and the many lead to great problems which are of the gravest import to humanity.

Community Defined. A community is a body of people having common interests and, usually, living in the same place, under the same laws and regulations. From the beginning of time, individuals have associated and grouped themselves into communities. Every Church is a community of believers. The Church which conforms to the whole law is the one characterized by authority and operating under authoritative laws.

The Individual in the Community. A community is a great organism, with individuality which must express itself in adaptation or opposition to law.

Since the community is composed of individuals, each with independent wills and agencies, nothing must be done, as a community, to prevent the full unfolding of the individual, for the more progressive the individuals, the more progressive is the community. While the community is under responsibility to each individual, the individual, having accepted a place and life in the community, must not do anything that will restrain other individuals of the community. Whatever is good for the many, must always take preference. This does not interfere, in the least, with full individual development, since the greatest individual development always comes from proper adaptation to law. When each individual faithfully obeys the law, the community is safe.

The Rights of the Community. The community has rights which are as inalienable as the free agency of individuals. An individual who will not obey the community laws should move out of the community. Those who remain must yield obedience to the laws established for the public good. This was well brought out in the Great Council, when Lucifer fell because he was not one with the community. In that great day, as in our day, the many had the right to demand that their good be considered as of primary importance.

Training for the Community. In view of the supremacy of the community it becomes indispensable that the powers of the individual be so unfolded as to be of service to the community. No man can selfishly stand aside and say "I am sufficient unto myself; in the community I have no interest; though I obey its laws, I do not serve it." It is not sufficient that a man obey the laws of the community; he must vigorously serve the community. Every act of every man's life must relate itself to the good of other men. This is fundamental in the Gospel, and should be fundamental in the daily relations of men.

This justifies the modern training now given men for the necessary pursuits and common tasks of daily life. Whatever is necessary, may and should be made honorable and dignified. All pursuits are made professional, so that all who serve the good of the many, may find the same joy in their work whatever it may be.   All men should be trained for service to the community.

It is an interesting commentary on the present-day Church that President Brigham Young was one of the first men in America to establish schools in which the training of men for the actual affairs of life was made pre-eminent. Today we train for citizenship, whether in the Church or in the State. In such training lies the hope of the community for its future. By such training will a feeling of community responsibility be established among men.

The Supremacy of the Community.   From all this and from what has been said in preceding chapters, it is clear that the Great Plan was so devised that men may unitedly work out their salvation. Man may not stand alone. Brotherhood is the great principle on which the Church is based.

Man and Nature.

CHAPTER 31.

MAN AND NATURE.

There is but one nature. All things, visible or invisible, belong to the one universe.

The Intelligence of Nature. Each and all of the numerous forces in the universe may be subjected to the will of man. In the universe are untold numbers of intelligent beings, whose main business it is to discover the ways of nature, and by an intelligent control of nature, to acquire greater power of advancing development. The holy spirit fills all things, and by its means the thoughts and minds of these increasing intelligent beings are everywhere felt. Intelligence permeates the universe.

The question is often asked, "Does nature, as we know it, the rocks and trees and beasts, possess intelligence of an order akin to that of man?" Who knows? That intelligence is everywhere present is beyond question. By the intelligent God, nature is directed. The forming of a crystal or the conception of a living animal is, somehow, connected with an intelligent purpose and will. This fruitful field of conjecture should be touched with care, for so little definite knowledge concerning it is in man's possession.

A Living Earth. It seems to be well established that the earth as a whole, is a living organism. It had a beginning; it will die or be changed, and after is purification it will be brought into greater glory as a resurrected organism. Even the symbolism of baptism was performed for the earth when the waters descended in the great flood. All this can simply mean that the earth, as well as all on it, are subject to the fundamental Plan, involving the atonement of Jesus Christ.

The earth as an organism does its work perfectly well. It is without sin. "The earth abides the law of a celestial kingdom, for it fills the measure of its creation, and transgresses not the law. Wherefore it shall be sanctified; yea, notwithstanding it shall die, it shall be quickened again, and shall abide the power by which it is quickened, and the righteous shall inherit it." If the earth is a living organism, it seems more than likely that all things on earth possess a measure of life and intelligence.

The Lower Animals. The lower animals were created by the power of God. All things created by him, have first been created spiritually, then temporally, after which they pass again into the spiritual life. Animals were created spiritually before they were given material existence. If the meaning of this doctrine is that animals lived before this, they certainly may live hereafter. That which is essential in animals is probably indestructible. Our knowledge of this subject is extremely limited, and whatever is said about it, is conjectural and subject to revision.

All for the Use of Man. Nevertheless, rocks and trees and beasts, are for the use of man, to be used by him in moderation and with wisdom. Man is at the head of the creations on earth. It is his duty to make proper use of them all. Whoever teaches that any part of the universe is not for the benefit of man, is in error.

Man's Conquest of Nature. It is the simplest of present-day doctrines that the vastness of nature makes it impossible for man to comprehend more than the minutest part of it. Yet, in the true philosophy of life, nothing is more certain than that the greatest mystery of nature may at some time be understood. The great purpose of man's existence is a complete understanding of all the mysteries of nature. True, the understanding that will give him full mastery over nature will come little by little. In the end, man shall know all that he desires. Even in that happy day he shall not be able to change one law of nature; only by intelligent control may he apply nature's laws to desired ends. With this certainty man may go onward hopefully. Nature is inexhaustible and man shall not, in all the endless ages, explore it completely; he shall only in the eternal days become more conscious of its infinite majesty—thereby comes the everlasting joy of man. Great hope of conquest enables man to meet his daily tasks, with lifted head and fearless courage. Man knows that all his search shall be successful, if he only search with might and main and have patience to wait.

Miracles. Man is of limited power; whatever he can not understand or duplicate may be called miraculous; and only in that sense can miracles be allowed. The miracles of the Savior were done only by superior knowledge. Nothing is unnatural. All that has been done, man may do as he increases in power. The conception of intelligence guiding the destinies of men, makes it possible that, in our behalf, wonderful things are often done, that transcend our understanding, but which are yet in full and complete harmony with the laws of nature. For ourselves we must discover all of nature that we can. In time of need, when our own knowledge does not suffice, the Master may give his help. Thus, after man has used his full knowledge and failed, the sick may be healed, the sorrowing, comforted, or wealth or poverty may come, provided we draw heavily enough upon the unseen forces about us. Help so obtained is not unnatural. A miracle is simply that which we can not understand, and at which we marvel.

Harmony of Man and Nature. Vast, unnumbered forces lie about us. The possible power of man, as he grows in knowledge, is quite beyond our under standing. All that is required of man is that he place himself in harmony with the interacting forces, operating in all directions. If the forces are not fully understood, he must search them out, and as best he can, must place himself so that they are with him rather than against him. To enjoy nature is our privilege and duty. No life finds joy above its harmonious associations with the things that lie about it in nature. All this is merely in accord with the fundamental doctrines already laid down. The Church possessing the truth, always fosters, encourages and respects all honest investigation of nature.

Man and Himself.

CHAPTER 32.

THE SOUND BODY.

Consideration has been given, in the preceding chapters, to the pre-existent life, the course of the Gospel on the earth, and man's relationship to God, to the Church and to his fellowman. Man must, also, give respectful consideration to himself, as an individual.

The Importance of the Body. Attention has already been called to the fact that the condition of the body limits, largely, the expression of the spirit. The spirit shines through the body only as the body permits. The body is essentially of the earth; and, in the earth career, the earthly envelope of the spirit would naturally determine the expression of man's powers. If the body is in poor condition from birth, man must strengthen it as the days increase; if it is strong from the beginning, he must make it stronger.

Food. A first consideration for the proper maintenance of bodily health, is the proper feeding of the body. Man should use food adapted to the body and seasonable according to nature. In accordance with the Word of Wisdom, meat should be used sparingly, and no food should be used to excess.

Exercise. The elimination of unassimilated food from the human body is quite as important as the taking in of food. For that purpose, physical exercise must be taken regularly. Moreover, exercise develops and strengthens all parts of

9

the body.   Manual labor, which usually is looked
upon as inferior to mental labor, is in reality a
means of improving the body, permitting hard mental labor and making possible a fuller expression of
man's spirit.   Man's life should not be given wholly
to physical work, but it should constitute a vital
part of it.

Rest.   Just as necessary as is food or exercise, is
the change called rest.   If the same muscles be exercised continuously they will surely tire and good
work can, then, no longer be done with them.   Regular rest should be given the body.   Frequently, a
change from one kind of work to another is a sufficient rest; but in many cases, cessation from effort
is necessary to recuperate man's strength, properly.
The natural law requiring regular sleep should be
obeyed, though none should sleep too long.   One
day out of seven, the Sabbath, should be devoted,
particularly, to matters concerning God and the
spiritual life, which too often are submerged during
the other days, in the material affairs of life.   An
occasional fasting is very desirable, since, for a few
hours, it gives some organs of the body a complete
rest.   At present, the Church practice is to fast
twenty-four consecutive hours once each month.
The food thus saved, in conformity with the fundamental spirit of brotherhood, is distributed among
those who have need of it, by ward officers specially
appointed for that purpose.

Stimulants.   In normal health, food, exercise,
rest, love of God and fellowman and daily work,
furnish a natural and sufficient stimulation for all
the duties of life.   In fact, none other should be
allowed, if the best physical health is to be retained.

Therefore, alcohol in all its forms, tobacco, tea, coffee and the variety of drugs should not be used. There is double danger in the use of stimulants: first, they tend to undermine the strength of the man, and, second, they take away from man his mastery of himself. Under the influence of a drug, man is urged on by the drug itself, and not by his own strength of will. This is most dangerous. A man who loses control of himself, never knows just what he may do.

Moral Purity. The body is much concerned in the moral purity of the man. Men and women must keep themselves pure or there will be a loss of life and procreative power. Moreover, men must keep themselves as pure as do women. No reasoning, based on natural law, justifies two standards of morality, one for the man and the other for the woman.

The Gospel and the Sound Body. The sound body is a Gospel requirement, for only with a sound body can man work out his mission and have full joy. Working effectively and to make others happy, can be done only in a healthy body. Every effort should be made to keep our bodies as sound as possible. It is a part of a rational theology.

CHAPTER 33.

EDUCATION FOR THE INNER LIFE.

After all, the body is only the tabernacle of the spirit. The spirit within, the essential part of man, must be developed as much as possible during the earth career.

The Senses. Knowledge is the material on which the mind works. In every progressive life fresh knowledge must be gathered as the days go by. The senses of man are the gateways through which that knowledge enters. The senses of man must be developed, therefore, as completely as is possible. Seeing, hearing, tasting, smelling and feeling must all be developed fully and joyously for the pleasure and benefit of man. Without sharp senses, man may not have the highest earthly joy.

The Reasoning Power. It is not sufficient for the contentment of man that he gather knowledge, and add fact to fact. All new information must be compared with other information, so that conclusions may be drawn, and new knowledge brought into view. By this process of reasoning, on the basis of acquired knowledge, man may rise by sure steps to a high degree of understanding. Man must train himself, with all his might, to use this wonderful faculty of reason, so that he may intelligently read new knowledge from all he learns. A fact, of itself, is lifeless; only when it is compared with other facts, does it leap into life, and show forth its hidden meaning.

The Feelings. The sense of feeling is but a poor expression for the one great sense by which man may directly communicate with the region of the unseen. Through this sense, man stands on the border line between earth and the external universe. Those who have communion with the forces about them, because of their greater refinement of feeling, have comfort which is attainable in no other manner.

Moreover, our feelings with respect to our fellow men should be cultivated. We must learn to sympathize with them in their distresses, rejoice with them in their joys, and pity them in their sins. The education of the feelings is a great duty of man.

The Spiritual Sense. This sense is closely akin to the feelings. The virtues of man, such as hope, charity, and mercy, can reach high development only on the basis of the conviction that the unseen world may be known. When this conviction grows upon a man, and he reaches out for a fuller understanding of it, his spiritual sense develops, new worlds are opened to him and he conforms to the intelligent love which made the Great Plan possible.

Symbolism. Moreover, as man develops, he learns to be content to know eternal truths only in great symbols. That is, he learns to be satisfied to know that he does not fully know. This has already been dwelt upon and need not be further emphasized. The Sacrament, as an ordinance of the Church is one of the great symbols of the suffering and death of Jesus for the sake of mankind, that the Great Plan might be fulfilled. Bread is eaten and water is drunk as symbols of the body and blood of the Savior, given in the atoning sacrifice. Every other ordinance is similarly symbolic. Back of the symbols lies the whole Great Plan in all of its gradations. God demands that the sacrament be partaken of frequently, so that the atoning sacrifice of Jesus may be held before the people continually; so with the other great symbols of the Church. By them the realities of eternal life are held before us.

Education. The whole of life is education, or training for further work. No wonder, therefore, that, in the correct philosophy of life, schools and other devices for the training of man's powers are foremost. Education is and must be carried onward fully and abundantly, in the Church of Christ. The support of education is, indeed, a test of the truthfulness of the Church.

CHAPTER 34.

SATISFACTION WITH DAILY WORK.

All must work—in defense if for no other reason. Without some kind of labor, body and mind will deteriorate. Clearly, however, all cannot do the same work, unless each man does practically all the variety of work necessary for the production of the things necessary in his life. In a complex civilization of many needs, that would be impossible or wasteful. The great satisfaction of earth-life is to be content with whatever work may come.

Variety of Earthly Tasks. In obedience to God's command, man must devote himself to the work of subduing the earth. This is no simple task, for the earth is an organism of many elements. Moreover, the needs of man are varied and manifold, to the satisfying of which, the subjection of the earth is ordained. There is an endless variety of tasks, for body and mind, to be accomplished by the men and women of earth. These tasks differ greatly; some concern themselves chiefly with the body; others, chiefly with the mind; and yet others with both body and mind. Some deal with this, and others with that, essential need; some with this, and others with that, necessary condition. The vocations of man are almost numberless. Much unhappiness has come to men because they have been obliged in life to follow one vocation when they would rather follow another. If a man thus be unhappy in his daily work the whole of his life is akin to failure, because he does not truly realize the possible joys of life. Occasionally, the discontent is due to the unwillingness of the man to earn his bread in the sweat of his brow. This is due to ignorance. Earnest, sincere labor, requiring steady and full effort, is the source of many abiding joys.

All Work May be Intelligent. If intelligence pervades all things, and if all things belong to the Great Plan, including the labors in which man lives and moves, then all tasks may and should be made intelligent and appealing to mind as well as to body. Rational as it is, it is however a relatively new thought, that to every task, if properly illumined by knowledge, many forces of the mind may be applied. As man has gained added knowledge, this has become more and more evident. The fact that intelligence may be made to illuminate the so-called humbler tasks, lifts much of the so-called curse from the labor of man. This is another reason for the education of man into an understanding of the full meaning of the necessary tasks of life. It justifies the support of research into all divisions of nature, and stamps with approval honest study and investigation of every kind. All kinds of work must be done; full preparation for every kind of work is fully justified.

Nothing Temporal. God has never given a temporal commandment. All God's creative works are first spiritual, then temporal. That is, they were first begotten of the intelligent mind, and must represent some necessity in the Great Plan. Whatever, therefore, is brought into operation on earth for the good of man, must represent great, eternal, spiritual realities. In conformity with this thought, every task,

however apparently humble, however apparently re-
mote from fundamental principles, has a spiritual
counterpart, and is necessary for the completion of
the plan under which man works. It matters little,
therefore, whether man devote his life to the tilling of
the soil, the making of shoes or the writing of books,
so that the work be well done. All such tasks are
proper, dignified and necessary parts of the Great
Plan, and will lead man along the path of eternal
progression. This means that, no matter to what
work a man may give himself, providing it is honorable and he do it with all his might, he may rest secure that on the last great day, the work will be
transmuted into spiritual values, and as such will be
written into the eternal record. The quality and not
the kind of work is the final test of man's achieve-
ments.

Man knows relatively little. He accepts his part
without knowing its meaning in the full economy of
God's plan for his children. Wise is the man who
spends his strength, with a full heart, in the accomplishment of the nearest work. He will find his work
transmuted into things glorious beyond his dreams.
More than that: Man need not wait long for the
transmutation of his honest work. Strength comes
to the man of honest and full endeavor, irrespective
of the kind of work, and on this earth his efforts
are transmuted into a great and noble joy. All
work is holy, and, well done, will bring its own
reward, here and in the hereafter.

Without question, men should seek the work they
think they love best, or for which they are best fitted.
Yet, the majority of men can do most work in a
satisfactory manner. The work that we finally must

do, we should accept in the light of its eternal value.

Subjection of Self. Nevertheless, to accept a place in society—not always the place one desires; to do well the work that is near at hand—not always the work one wishes; to love and to cherish the work, and to forget oneself in the needs of others, all that is not always easy. Such a life means a subjection of self which can be accomplished only if there is a clear understanding of the plan of salvation.

CHAPTER 35.

THE HOPE OF TOMORROW.

Time is unceasing. There was a yesterday, there is a today, and there will be a tomorrow. The Gospel plan encompasses all time. Tomorrow has a great place in the eternal plan.

Today. The greatest day of all time is today. It is the product of all the past; and is the promise of all the future. If each today is made great, the tomorrows will be surpassingly greater. The one way to draw out of life the keen joys of life, is to think little of tomorrow, but to live mightily today.

Tomorrow. Yet, surely, there will be a tomorrow. The sun sets, and we sleep, and we awaken to a new day. Forever there shall come new days. Today is our great day; but there will be another great, a greater day. What tomorrow shall be, depends measureably upon today. At least, the beginning of tomorrow will be as the evening of today. As we spend today, so will the hope of tomorrow be. The ages do not come in leaps, but step by step do they enter into the larger life.

The law of today is that joy will transfigure each coming tomorrow, if our work be well done today. No man knows whether his tomorrow will be on this earth or in another existence, with new duties and under a new environment. Of one thing we are sure, beyond all cavil, that life on earth will continue into an endless future, and the work will be taken up where it was laid down yesterday.

The Resurrection. The man whose life is ordered right, worries little about his tomorrow. Full well he knows that, though the body be laid in the grave, it will rise again. He has the absolute assurance of the resurrection. In that resurrection the body will arise purified, possessing only its essential, characteristic parts, which cannot be taken away or transferred to another body. These essential, characteristic parts organized into a body will be the mortal body made immortal.

The resurrection of mortal bodies, on earth, began with Jesus, who on the third day rose from the grave, and after his sojourn among the children of men, took his body with him into heaven. This was the first fruit of the resurrection, made possible by the atonement of the Christ. Since that time, the resurrection of man may have continued, and no doubt will continue, in the future; for many spirits have laid down their earthly bodies, and all must be raised from the grave. In the resurrection, order and law will prevail, and the just deserts of men will be kept in mind.

Our Place in the Hereafter. Into a new, great world shall we enter after the journey on earth has ended. In this new world we shall continue our work of progression, forever and forever, under the prevailing laws. Our progress, there, and the laws revealed to us, will depend upon our own actions and upon our own willingness to abide by the laws already known to us.

Our place in that life will depend on our faithfulness here. Whatever a man has gained on earth, will rise with him in the resurrection. All that he gained in the spirit world, before he came on earth, will likewise rise with him. All men will be saved, but the degree of that salvation will vary even as our varying work on earth. There will be glory upon glory, and there will be different degrees of advancement, some like unto the sun, some like unto the moon, while other glories will differ even as the infinite stars of the heavens differ in the brightness.

In the Great Plan there is no provision for the eternal damnation of man. At the best, men will be ranged according to their stage of progression—some higher, some lower. In a universe ruled by intelligent beings, filled with love for each other, there can be no thought of an endless damnation only as men, by opposition to law, destroy themselves. Endless punishment and eternal punishment, terms often used, but of little meaning to the human mind, mean simply God's punishment, which is beyond our understanding. Those who refuse to accept truth or to abide by law, will gradually take less and less part in the work of progression. They will be left behind, while their intelligent fellows, more obedient, will go on. In nature there is no standing still; those who do not advance, will retrograde, become weaker and finally wither, and be forgotten in their low estate.

The Destiny of Man. The intelligence called man cannot be destroyed. Eternal life is therefore the destiny of man. But, eternal life is life open-eyed, ready-minded, seeking, accepting and using all knowledge that will assist in man's progress. To continue forever, upward, that is eternal life and the destiny of man.

CHAPTER 36.

THE LAW OF THE EARTH.

In the high heavens yet hang the stars. Throughout the infinite universe still play the hosts of mighty forces. The full conquest of the earth by man is yet to be accomplished. As things were when man opened his eyes after birth, so do they appear to be today. Yet, during the years that have gone, the man has changed; for now he knows his origin and his destiny, and the purpose of his life on earth. He knows that throughout the seeming sameness there is progressive change; that, as he has changed, so has the world changed, too; that the all pervading Intelligent God of the universe is engaged in a progressive development.

Man has found his place amidst the things about him. Whence? Whither? He knows; and with smiling courage sets out to subdue the tasks of the day, knowing well that the day's labor, whatever it may be, in righteousness, shall count for him in the endless journey which he is making.

The Unknown Meaning. The man has learned that in an infinite universe, admitting of endless development, things may not be fully known. The very essence of things must forever be the goal, towards which intelligence strives. Nevertheless, man also knows that to approach by slow degrees, but steadily, the full knowledge which gives unmeasured power over natural forces, is the way of progress.

So he is content to let each day speak one new word of the unknown meaning of the universe.

The universe is one. All things in it are parts of one whole. The dominating spirit of the vastness of space and of its contents is the dominating spirit of the least part of that which constitutes the whole. It matters not then, to what a man give himself. In everything and anything may the riddle of the universe be read, if the search be continued long enough. Modest in his possessions, yet courageous in his hope of ultimate conquest, he stands before the things of his life, small or great, knowing of a surety that in them lie the truths that overwhelm the universe.

"Flower in the crannied wall,
I pluck you out of the crannies,
I hold you here, root and all, in my hand,
Little flower—but if I could understand
What you are, root and all, and all in all,
I should know what God and man is."

Knowing all this, and the outline of his origin and destiny, man must be forever engaged in extending the philosophy, in accordance with which he orders and guides his life.

The Earth-Law. On earth the man dwells today. Great are the conceptions revealed to him concerning the constitution, progress and destiny of the universe. Marvelous to his understanding is the knowledge of his full and vital place in the scheme of things. Yet, encompassed by earth conditions, he strives to assemble all this vast, divine and wondrous knowledge, and out of it to draw some simple formula, in the language of man, that may be applied in

the affairs of earth, and which shall be a simple
guide to him in all that he may do.

Such a formula was sought and found by the first
man, and has been used by the righteous of all ages.
In the meridian of time, when Jesus of Nazareth,
the Christ, came upon earth to fulfil the central
thought in the plan of salvation, he stated the formula in words that never have been surpassed. Thus
runs the formula, and thus is worded the law of the
earth: "Thou shalt love the Lord thy God with
all thy heart; and with all thy soul and with all thy
mind. Thou shalt love thy neighbor as thyself. On
these two commandments hangeth the law and the
prophets."

This, in short, is man's duty while he dwells in the
flesh. His God, his fellowman and himself—the
three concerns of his life. We say it is the earth-law,
but like all other things of the earth, it stands for
huge spiritual meanings, and is therefore an eternal
law for all times and for all places.

To Love God. What does it mean, to love God
with one's heart and soul and mind? Certainly, a love
of the heart and the soul and the mind can not be
given to a Being who is not known nor understood.
Such love is more than a blind obedience. In such
a love there must be a rational understanding of
God's nature and of his place in the universe and of
his relation to men. There must be in such a fulness
of love an acceptance of God's superior knowledge, of
his intelligent Plan for man and of his supreme and
final authority. Such a love can not well be forgotten
or survive, unless God is part of a universe, the
orderly outlines of which can be fathomed by the
human mind. That such knowledge may be pos-

sessed by man, and that a real unfeigned love for God may be developed, has been taught in the preceding pages. Neither can God be fully loved unless he is obeyed; and the first command is simple, "Multiply and replenish the earth and subdue it."

To Love a Neighbor as Oneself. To love oneself —that is easy. Instinctively, from the first day, we have reached out for our own greater good. Every personal philosophy makes the man the center. To love our neighbor equally well—"that's the rub." His will is not our will; his ways, not our ways. Yet, only by the progress of all, can each gain the greatest advancement. The fundamental conceptions of a universe filled with eternal matter and forces, and a host of individual intelligent beings, make it clear that only by complete harmony of all intelligent beings can the interests of each be served, in the work of subjugating, by intelligent conquest, the forces of universal nature.

To love one's neighbor, then, a man must first know fully his own origin and destiny and possible powers; then he may soon learn the need of loving his fellowman, if his love for himself shall grow great. This commandment is not inferior to the first.

The Triumph of Man. The eternal, conscious, willing being, having become an earthly man, stands before the law of the earth. If he strives, all the days of his life, to bring into perfect accord, the God who rules, his earthly brother and himself, he will at length win the victory in the battle of his life. Out of such a life will come, among other gifts, controlled personal desires, subjection to law, a recognition of the great power of man, and the harmonious adjustment of contending forces to the completion of the Great Plan which governs man's earth-life. Whether living or dead, such a person has triumphed, and the journey from the dim beginning has not been in vain. To such souls comes the reward of the unspeakable joy of a perfect understanding of the meaning of life, and the living peace that passeth understanding—through which appears the vital future, ever vigorously progressing towards an increasing, virile goal.

Have you tried the virtue of the law of the earth? If you have not, try it now, for it is good.

Appendix.

The doctrines and views set forth in the preceding pages, based on the teachings of the elders of the Church, especially of the Prophet Joseph Smith, may be confirmed by a study of the doctrinal standards of the Church, namely, the Bible, the Book of Mormon, the Doctrine and Covenants and the Pearl of Great Price. The following references, chosen almost at random, from these standards, especially from the Doctrine and Covenants, are for the immediate use of those who wish to pursue the study somewhat more in detail. For a critical study, an exhaustive examination must necessarily be made of the doctrinal standards and of the mass of books and printed sermons on the system of belief of the Church of Jesus Christ of Latter-day Saints. Such students will find the existing indexes or concordances to the standard authorities of most value,* but they will also obtain much ready help from the several existing excellent compilations of references, classified under doctrinal headings.† A list of Church literature may be obtained from the Deseret News and Deseret Sunday School Union Bookstores, Salt Lake City, Utah.

REFERENCES.

CHAPTERS 1 AND 2

    Doctrine and Covenants 1:28; 42:61; 46:18; 84:19; 88: 78-80, 118, 119; 89:19; 90:15; 93:11-14, 29-36, 53; 101:25; 128:14; 130:18, 19; 131:6.

CHAPTER 3

    Doctrine and Covenants 3:2; 9:7-9; 28:13; 29:31-35; 49:17; 76:13, 22-24; 82:4; 86:9; 88:13, 25, 26, 34-45; 93:21-23, 29; 105:5; 121:30-32; 130:20, 21; 131:7; 132:8.

Cruden's Concordance to the Bible (or some other good concordance). *A Complete Concordance to the Book of Mormon* (George Reynolds). *A Concordance to the Book of Doctrine and Covenants* (John A. Widtsoe). No index has as yet been made for the *Pearl of Great Price*, but the book is small and may be read easily in its entirety.

†*The Compendium* (Richards and Little) is the type after which most of the later compilations have been fashioned.

Pearl of Great Price, Abraham 3:18-21; Moses 1:33, 35; 3:5 9.

Book of Mormon, I Nephi 10:19; II Nephi 11:5; Alma 13:6, 7; 34:9; 42:16.

Bible, Job 38:4-7; Jer. 1:5; John 9:2; 17:5; Heb. 12:9; Rom. 6:23.

CHAPTER 4

Doctrine and Covenants 9:7-9;

Book of Mormon, Alma 12:11, 31; 29:4, 5; 30:9; Moroni 10:4, 5; Mosiah 18:28.

CHAPTER 5

Doctrine and Covenants, Lectures on Faith 7:8; sections 50:24; 93:12-14, 20; 132:20.

Book of Mormon, Alma 32:32; Mosiah 4:12.

CHAPTER 6

Doctrine and Covenants 3:2, 4, 10; 6:2; 76:2-4; 88:13, 41; 93:1, 12-15, 29-38; 107:54, 55; 110:1-4; 130:1-3, 22.

Pearl of Great Price, Abraham 4:1-31.

CHAPTER 7

Doctrine and Covenants 45:71; 58:18; 77:2; 88:15; 93:28, 33, 34; 98:8; 128:19; 133:33.

Book of Mormon, II Nephi 2:25; Enos 1:3; Ether 3:6-20.

CHAPTER 8

Doctrine and Covenants 9:3-6; 10:66; 18:11-13; 19:16-19; 29:35-42, 46; 58:28; 74:7; 76:25, 26, 39-41, 69; 93:29-39; 98:8; 101:78; 104:17; 121:32

Pearl of Great Price, Abraham 3:18, 25, 26.

Book of Mormon, I Nephi 4:33; 6:4; II Nephi 2:3, 6, 27; 9:5, 25-26; 10:23-25; 31:21; Alma 3:26; 7:12; 12:31; 13:3; Mosiah 3:5; 4:6-9; Helaman 14:30.

Bible, Gen. 2:17; Isa. 63:9; Matt. 18:11; John 1:29; 3:14, 15; 12:32; Rom. 3:25; 5:15; 6:23; I Tim. 2:5; Gal. 3:13; Jude 1:6; Rev. 12:7.

CHAPTER 9

Doctrine and Covenants 82:4; 88:35-40; 93:38; 128 sec.

Book of Mormon, I Nephi 10:18; 21:6; II Nephi 9:18, 25; Alma 12:25; 30:11; 34:16.

Bible Neh. 9:17; Acts 15:18.

CHAPTER 10

Doctrine and Covenants 27:11; 29:35-41; 38:1-3; 107:53, 54; 116:1.

Pearl of Great Price, Abraham chaps. 4 and 5.

Book of Mormon, II Nephi 2:9-25; Alma 12:22, 23, 31; 18:29; Mosiah 2:25; 3:16; 4:2; Mormon 9:12.

Bible, Gen. chap. 3; Rom. 5:12.

CHAPTER 11
  Pearl of Great Price, Book of Moses, Book of Abraham; Writings of Joseph Smith.
  Bible. Genesis; The Gospels.
CHAPTER 12
  Doctrine and Covenants 18:18; 19:24; 27:11; 29:34; 39:6; 50:43; 76:56-58; 78:15-18; 84:37, 38; 93:1-17; 107:53-56; 121:28-32; 132:19, 20, 23, 37.
  Pearl of Great Price, Abraham 3:1-5.
  Book of Mormon, Alma 12:31.
  Bible, Gen. 1:26; Deut. 10:17; Exo. 15:11; Psalms 86:8; Dan. 2:47; I Cor. 8:5; Rev. 17:14.
CHAPTER 13
  Doctrine and Covenants 5:2; 27:18; 29:30, 31; 59:14; 93:26; 95:4.
  Book of Mormon, I Nephi 1:12; II Nephi 2:4; Alma 7:13; Ether 2:15.
  Bible, Gen. 6:3; Prov. 1:23; Dan. 4:8; John 16:13.
CHAPTER 14
  Doctrine and Covenants 4:7; 9:8; 41:3; 42:16, 61; 46:28; 50:29; 59:14; 68:33; 89:18, 19; 121:26-33.
  Book of Mormon, II Nephi 21:2, 3; 31:3; Alma 11:41; 32:34; 34:39; Moroni 10:10.
CHAPTER 15
  Doctrine and Covenants 10:12, 23-33, 63; 29:28, 29, 36-40; 35:9; 52:14; 76:28; 84:67; 88:114; 121:4; 124:98; 129:8.
  Book of Mormon, II Nephi 2:17; III Nephi 13:12; 18:15; Mosiah 16:5; Moroni 7:12.
CHAPTER 16
  Doctrine and Covenants 10:67; 11:24-26; 20:1; 21:1-3; 22:3; 26:2; 29:42, 43; 41:2, 3; 42:8; 43:8; 45:14; 50:44; 58:23; 76:54; 115:4.
CHAPTER 17
  Faith
  Doctrine and Covenants, Lectures on Faith, sections 18:18; 35:9; 41:3; 44:2; 45:8; 49:11-14; 52:20; 85:1, 2; 136:42.
  Book of Mormon. I Nephi 10:6, 17; II Nephi 25:26; Enos 1:8; Mosiah 8:18; Ether 12:10.
  Bible, Genesis 15:6; Exodus 4:5; Numbers 20:12; Psalms 119:66 ;Prov. 16:20; John 5:24; 20:29; Acts 8:37; 10:43; II Cor. 5:7.
  Repentance
  Doctrine and Covenants 1:32, 33; 18:42; 20:29; 39:18; 90:34.

Book of Mormon, I Nephi 10:18; II Nephi 30:4; Alma
    12:24; 26:22; Mosiah 27:24.
Bible, Matt. 3:2; Luke 13:3; II Peter 3:9; Rev. 3:19.
Baptism
    Doctrine and Covenants 18:42; 20:37, 72-74; 55:2; 68:
        8, 25-27; 76:51; 128:12.
    Book of Mormon, Alma 28:18; Moroni 8:4-22.
    Bible, Matt. 28:19; Mark 16:16; Luke 3:3; John 1:33;
        3:23; I Cor. 12:13; Eph. 4:5.
Gift of the Holy Ghost
    Doctrine and Covenants 20:41; 33:15; 35:6; 76:52, 114-
        118; 121:26-32.
    Book of Mormon, Alma 31:36.
    Bible, Acts 8:17; 9:17; 19:2-6.
CHAPTER 18
    Doctrine and Covenants, Lectures on Faith. Sections
        18:27; 20:2, 3, 38-71; 27:1-18; 84:14-21, 35-39; 107:
        1-5, 40-52; 112:31, 32; 128:20.
    Book of Mormon, Mosiah 29:42; Alma 4:4; 6:1; 13:1-3,
        5-20; Helaman 8:18.
    Bible, Gen. 12:1-3; 13:14-18; Psalms 110:4; John 15:16;
        Acts 14:23; Heb. 2:17; 3:1; 4:14; 5:1; 7:3, 15-28;
        I Peter 2:5; Titus 1:5; II Tim. 1:6.
CHAPTER 19
    Doctrine and Covenants 20:60-67; 26:2; 28:13; 68:19-21;
        78:1; 104:21; 107, whole section; 124:123-145.
CHAPTER 20
    Doctrine and Covenants 84:18, 21, 35; 107:30-32; 113:8;
        121:36-46; 128:9-11; 132:28, 45-49.
    Book of Mormon, Alma 5:3; I Nephi 10:23.
CHAPTER 21
    Doctrine and Covenants 3.4; 6:9; 19:33; 20:20; 29,34;
        56:1; 58:21; 63:55; 64:34; 82:10; 88:22-39; 98:4-7;
        101:43-62; 103:31-34; 105:5; 124:49; 130:19, 20, 21;
        134, whole section.
    Book of Mormon, II Nephi 2:23, 27; 9:25; Alma 30:3,
        11; 42:17; Mosiah 5:8; 2:32-37; Moroni 8:25.
CHAPTER 22
    Doctrine and Covenants 1:1-2, 23; 4:5; 19:21, 22; 36:4-8;
        33:8-12; 38:11; 42:63; 45:20; 49:11-14; 84:87; 90:11;
        112:30.
CHAPTER 23
    Doctrine and Covenants 13:21; 36:8; 84:5; 105:33;
        109:5; 110:8; 124, whole section; 128:15, 24; 133:2.
    Book cf Mormon, II Nephi 5:6; 33:15; III Nephi 11:1;
        Jacob 1:17; Mosiah 1:18; 2:1-7; Alma 10:2; Hela-
        man 3:9; 10:7.

CHAPTER 24 ·
 Doctrine and Covenants 1:10; 38:24; 42:27; 59:6; 81:4;
  88:81; 136:20-27.
CHAPTER 25
 Book of Mormon, Jacob 5:66; Mosiah 27:3; 29:38;
  Alma 1:26.
CHAPTER 26
 Book of Mormon, II Nephi 26:30; 33:4; Mosiah 18:21;
  Ether 12:27.
CHAPTER 27
 Doctrine and Covenants 42:30-39, 53-55, 71-73; 51:1-20;
  44:6; 52:40; 78:1-2; 82:1-24; 83:1-6; 85:1-5, 9-12;
  92:1-2; 104:1-86; 105:34; 119:1-7.
 Book of Mormon, III Nephi 26:19; IV Nephi 1:2, 3, 16.
 Bible, Numbers 18:26-28; Lev. 27:30; II Chron. 31:5, 6;
  Neh. 10:37, 38; Mal. 3:18; Matt. 19:16-21; Luke
  18:12; Acts 4:31-32, 35; Heb. 7:5.
CHAPTER 28
 Doctrine and Covenants, sections 2 and 128; 21:1; 47:3;
  57:3; 93:8-17; 110:13-16; 124:33; 127:5-8; 128:2-5.
 Book of Mormon, II Nephi 26:30; Mosiah 2:4.
CHAPTER 29
 Doctrine and Covenants 18:42; 20:70, 71; section 25; 29:
  46, 47; 49:15-17; 55:4; 68:25-27; 74:5, 6; 83:4, 5; 84:27,
  28; 93:40-42; 131:2; section 132.
 Bible, Gen. 1:27; 15:5; 2:18, 23; 20:12; Deut. 7:3; I Cor.
  11:11.
CHAPTER 30
 Doctrine and Covenants 38:23; 50:40; 55:4; 69:7; 88:77,
  79, 118, 119, 127, 137; 90:8, 15; 93:53; 95:17; 130:19.
CHAPTER 31
 Doctrine and Covenants 20:17; 29:24, 31, 32; 45:58; 49:
  16, 19; 59:18, 21; 77:2, 3; 88:20-45; 89:15; 103:7;
  130:9.
 Book of Mormon, II Nephi 8:6; Ether 6:4; 13:9.
CHAPTER 32
 Doctrine and Covenants 42:24; 49:19-21; 59:14-20;
  63:16; 88:124; section 89; 132:41.
CHAPTER 34
 Doctrine and Covenants 29:32-35.
CHAPTER 35
 Doctrine and Covenants 18:12; 29:26-28; 45:45-54; 63:
  20, 21, 49: section 76; 77:1; 88:14-42; 101:25, 78;
  130:9-11.

Book of Mormon, Mosiah 16:9.
Bible, Daniel 12:2; Job 19:25; Luke 24:34; Rom. 8:24;
     Rev. 1:18; 20:5, 6.
CHAPTER 36
Book of Mormon, Mosiah 23:15.
Bible, Matt. 22:34-40.

Index.

CPSIA information can be obtained
at www.ICGtesting.com
Printed in the USA
LVHW081052070520
655170LV00015B/171